The Silent Explosion

The Silent Explosion

by Philip Appleman

With a Foreword by Sir Julian Huxley

BEACON PRESS   BOSTON

The author gratefully acknowledges permission to reprint passages from *America;* "Man, the Destroying Biotype," by Raymond Bouillenne, *Science,* Vol. 135, 2 March 1962, pp. 706-712; *The Challenge of Man's Future* by Harrison Brown, The Viking Press Inc., Publishers, 1954; "Americans Wonder" by Vladimir Mayakovsky, *Anthology of Russian Literature in the Soviet Period,* edited by Bernard Guerney, Random House, Inc., copyright © 1960; *Report from Palermo* by Danilo Dolci, The Orion Press, Inc., 1961; *The Biology of Human Starvation* by Ancel Keys, Josef Brozek, Austin Henschel, Olaf Mickelsen, and Henry Longstreet Taylor, University Press, University of Minnesota, Copyright 1950 by the University of Minnesota; *The New York Times;* statements by Lammot du Pont Copeland and Adolph W. Schmidt, Planned Parenthood–World Population; *And the Poor Get Children* by Lee Rainwater, copyright © 1960 by Social Research, Inc., and published by Quadrangle Books, Chicago; *Bird of Sorrow* by Rev. John Romaniello, M.M., P. J. Kenedy & Sons; *Antigone* by Sophocles, trans. by Dudley Fitts and Robert Fitzgerald, Harcourt, Brace & World, Inc., 1949; *Commonweal.*

*To my colleagues and students in
The International School of America,
1960–1961, 1962–1963,
and to my wife*

Preface

In 1960-1961 and 1962-1963 I was privileged to teach a course in World Literature and Philosophy in the International School of America, a unique educational institution that annually, since 1959, has flown a small group of college students and their professors around the world to visit and study sixteen countries over a regular academic year. The object of the I.S.A. is to examine various cultures and world conditions at first hand. It is always a profoundly instructive experience. Those two intense years of study, observation, and discussion are at the heart of this book.

I want to thank the Administration of Indiana University for generously allowing me leaves of absence; Karl Jaeger, Executive Director of the International School of America, for conceiving the school, bringing it into existence, and maintaining it; and my I.S.A. colleagues and students, whose cooperation and challenge were a source of growth for me as a scholar, a writer, and a person.

I also want to thank the Conservation Foundation, the Indiana University Foundation, and the Huntington Hartford Foundation for their generous support; and the Population Reference Bureau for checking statistical data.

I am especially grateful to those who have read all or parts of the manuscript. Not all of them agree with everything in it, but all have offered valuable suggestions: C. L. Barber, Robert C. Cook, Robert S. Davis, Paul Dietl, Wallace W. Douglas, Dean Fraser, Harold Hill, Sir Julian Huxley, George Levine, John Liell, William A. Madden, Herbert J. Muller, Samuel H. Ordway, Jr., The Rev. John Powell, S.J., John Rock, Karl Sax, George Stolnitz, Joseph Sutton, Michael Wolff, and my wife.

P. A.

Bloomington, Indiana
November, 1964

Contents

Foreword

Professor Appleman's book deserves to be widely read. He and his students saw with their own eyes the poverty and misery, the apathy and frustration, brought about by overpopulation—in Calcutta streets, in remote Indian villages, in the shacks and floating slums of Hong Kong, even in fertile Thailand.

The Silent Explosion brings home with vividness and cogency the moral implications for the United States (and, I would add, for all other scientifically and technologically advanced nations) of the so-called population explosion. He particularly stresses (and here I am in fullest agreement with him) the moral responsibility of the U.S. government to devote large amounts of money and brains to research on human reproduction and its control, and to make the results freely and fully available to all governments (and, of course, to responsible medical and social organizations) concerned with the problems of maternal health, family planning, and population control. Not to accept this responsibility is to be immoral, and immoral on the grand scale—it condemns millions more human beings to an increasingly wretched existence.

He also brings out the economic and social implications of the population explosion. The urgent economic need of densely populated underdeveloped countries is industrialization. But to achieve industrialization, massive capital investment is necessary—of money, machinery, and human skill and devotion. If the rate of population increase is too high, so much of the financial, material, and human capital will be used up in feeding, housing, educating, and caring for the new crop of human beings that there will not be enough left to achieve the breakthrough to a viable industrial economy. As Coale and Hoover* have pointed out, too rapid population increase may bring a country

---

* Ansley J. Coale and Edgar M. Hoover, *Population Growth and Economic Development in Low-Income Countries* (Oxford, 1959).

to a point of no return, and its last state may be worse than its first.

This has a lesson for all grant-giving and loan-making and aid-providing agencies. If a recipient country's population is growing too fast, aid may be wholly wasted, or may even aggravate the economic and social situation. Aid-giving agencies should regard it as their duty to enquire into the "demographic credit-worthiness" of the applicant; if this is not satisfactory, then aid should be conditional on the recipient country's taking steps to control the growth of its population, and part of the aid should be utilized to implement any such efforts.

Professor Appleman also brings out into the open the wrongheadedness and indeed the essential wrongness of the ideological objections, both Marxist and Roman Catholic, to adequate population control. It is a strange irony that the Catholic Church and organized communism should here be standing shoulder to shoulder, and should be united only in an attitude which opposes necessary progress and tends to produce increasing human misery. I was particularly shocked by the pronouncement of the Catholic society in London, quoted by Professor Appleman on page 83, which regards the prevailing of "the Catholic race" (*sic*), as against the Protestants, as apparently the highest goal.

The only ideological consideration that ought to enter into this grave and indeed overwhelming problem is that of human fulfillment as against human frustration and misery, advance as against degradation, the fuller realization of human possibilities as against their restriction. The special value of Professor Appleman's book is that it reveals the moral nature of the population problem. Population increase is forcing man as a species to rethink his morality.

JULIAN HUXLEY

The Silent Explosion

The life of Man is a long march through the night, surrounded by in-visible foes, tortured by weariness and pain, towards a goal that few can hope to reach, and where none may tarry long. One by one, as they march, our comrades vanish from our sight, seized by the silent orders of omnipotent Death. Very brief is the time in which we can help them, in which their happiness or misery is decided.

—*Bertrand Russell,*
"A Free Man's Worship"

If anyone has the world's goods and sees his brother in need, yet closes his heart against him, how does God's love abide in him?

—*I John 3:17*

Chapter 1

A Million More Mouths Each Week

Are there not thousands in the world . . .
Who love their fellows even to the death,
And feel the giant agony of the world . . . ?

— JOHN KEATS[1]

At Sealdah Station, Calcutta, misery radiates outward. In the station, displaced families from East Pakistan hover around little piles of possessions. Outside, dusty streets straggle away in every direction, lined with tiny shacks built of metal scraps, pieces of old baskets, strips of wood, and gunny sacks. In the dark interiors of the shacks, small fires glow through the smoke, and dark faces gaze out at children playing in the urinous-smelling, fly-infested streets. In a few years the children who survive these conditions will stop playing and become adults; that is, they will grow taller and thinner and stand in the streets like ragged skeletons, barefoot, hollow-eyed, blinking their apathetic stares out of gray, dusty faces. That is not a bright future, but it is the only one many of these children can expect.

A visiting American student described his response to this sight: "I thought I was prepared for poverty. But to see men, women, and children sleeping on the sidewalks, looking like little bundles of rags, to see thousands of people living in shacks, like animals . . ." Another student finished his thought: "Once when I was stopped by a woman begging, I gathered all my courage and looked straight into her eyes, and it hit me then—these are *people*, like ourselves, and they have a right to live better than this." "About Asia," a third student reflected, "What I'll remember best is not its history but its misery."

Misery: traveling in Asia, you see it everywhere—in Jericho,

3

Bangkok, Delhi, and Cairo; in Hong Kong in the thousands of squatters' shacks, without water or sanitation, or in the miles of tenements where dozens of people live in a single room; and in the acres of sampans and junks crowded together to form the strange floating cities of the Orient, dark, dense aquatic jungles of bamboo and fluttering rags and people. Dr. Johnson's verdict still applies to those parts of the world: "Human life is everywhere a state in which much is to be endured, and little to be enjoyed."

The agony of the world has a long pedigree. "Man that is born of woman is of few days, and full of trouble," Job complained; "He cometh forth like a flower, and is cut down." "Nothing that hurts," cried Aeschylus' Prometheus, "can come with a new face." "Birth is suffering, decay is suffering, death is suffering," said the Buddha in his first sermon. Man's pilgrimage through this valley of tears has characteristically been weary, stale, flat, and unprofitable, nasty, brutish, and short.

Ironically, the world's poverty and misery are now most heavily concentrated in the lands of dark-skinned peoples whose ancestors had raised brilliant civilizations when the light-skinned Europeans were still comparatively barbarous. The Egyptians developed a complex and viable society thousands of years before the ancient Greeks. The splendid Gupta dynasty in India flourished five hundred years before Charlemagne. The Khmers developed a sophisticated civilization in Southeast Asia before William the Conqueror invaded England. The sumptuous Chinese cultures of the T'ang and Sung dynasties stretched over six centuries before the discovery of the New World. The Mayas, Toltecs, Aztecs, and Incas built brilliant empires in Latin America long before Europeans came.

Time, the great destroyer, eventually leveled all this ancient grandeur. Exhausted by wars, retrenched in traditional forms and customs, skeptical of the European Renaissance and Industrial Revolution, dominated and exploited by colonial Powers, the dark-skinned people did not "develop"; and their poverty-stricken lands gradually became, as Kipling once called them, "the dark places of the earth," seeming to have been "created by Providence in order to supply picturesque scenery."

That, unfortunately, is how Americans too often continue

to think of them. I do not mean only that a few thoughtless tourists can look upon half-starved "natives" and pronounce them "picturesque." What is worse is that from our land of refrigerators, television, automobiles, and air conditioning, even people of good will cannot conceive of Asian poverty and misery.

There are poor people in the United States, of course; thirty million Americans live in varying degrees of poverty. We have our slums and shantytowns, our run-down marginal farms, our half-deserted mining areas, our disadvantaged groups: minorities, the very young workers, the very old, the chronically ill, the dropouts, the migrants. All of these share some degree of discomfort, some of them a steady and terrible misery. But without minimizing the cruel suffering of many of our own poor, it ought to be recognized that standards of poverty vary. An American family of four is considered poor if it has an annual income of less than three thousand dollars.[2] The *average* (not the "poor") family in underdeveloped countries gets about one-tenth of that. Even an out-of-work American may take home more money in unemployment compensation in a month than many working men in the underdeveloped countries earn in a whole year. Our relief and charitable organizations (unlike those in the underdeveloped countries) are not only well financed but also able to draw upon vast stores of surplus commodities. During the Great Depression itself we in this country were surrounded by the paradox of badly distributed abundance.

In Latin America, Asia, and Africa, on the other hand, poverty has a grim and simple meaning: there is just not enough to go around. An Indian eats about half as much food as an American does, partly because that is all he can afford and partly for the compelling reason that that is all there is for him. It is this perpetual scarcity, this fact of having *nowhere to turn*, that is so hard for Americans to understand—but until we do understand it, we will remain hopelessly out of touch with most of the world.

If we could somehow come to understand the meaning of this "giant agony," we would never again be complacent about it. When you walk the streets of Calcutta, you see gaunt and half-naked men bathing at public water taps; women huddling over little piles of manure, patting it into cakes for fuel; children

competing with dogs for refuse; hundreds of thousands of homeless people living in the streets, shaving in the streets, having
their teeth pulled in the streets, and sleeping in the streets. See-
ing this scene for the first time, Westerners react with shock,
shame, and revulsion. American students told me:

> I wanted to run away, to weep. I was disgusted, horrified, sad-
> dened. How I wished I were back in my secure and satisfying home.
> My heart and thoughts were thrown into turmoil and confusion.

> The first emotion this poverty evoked from me was shame—
> shame that I had so much, that I have been so lucky, that I could
> board a plane and leave all this. I felt I should be in the streets with
> them, begging.

> To associate with these slum-dwellers is to go insane from pity
> and frustration; to ignore them is not only inhumane, it's impossible.
> Day after day this "life" goes on. What hope is there?

"What hope is there?" The unhappy answer is that, as of now,
there can be very little hope for improvement.

The reasons for the poverty of the underdeveloped countries are complicated; they stretch back into obscure pre-history
and out into the jigsaw relations of religion, law, education,
politics, economics, and social custom. But one reason conditions
are *staying* so persistently bad is that the populations of these
countries are growing much too rapidly. Demands—for everything—are increasing so fast that supplies cannot keep pace. It
takes only simple arithmetic to show that when a country's
population increases faster than its production, there are less and
less goods per consumer. The late Prime Minister Nehru of India
once wrote, "We can never plan for the nation . . . if the population grows at this rate."[3] Each year, growing at a rate of 2.2 per
cent, India adds a population greater than Sweden's to the
masses it already has. In many other parts of the underdeveloped
world, populations are growing at an even faster rate. The "population explosion" is not a vague menace of the distant future.
It is here and now.

In 1960 the population of the earth reached three billion.
It took tens of thousands of years for mankind to produce this
number; yet in about thirty-five more years—while most of the
children born in 1960 are still alive—there will almost certainly

be an *additional* three billion people on the earth. This incredible acceleration is unmanageable and malignant—more like cancer than like healthy growth. It will intensify the misery in the under-developed countries, for nations that cannot even now feed, clothe, house, and educate their people surely will not be able to satisfy so many more, so soon. Calcutta today, still swollen by millions of refugees until the streets are spotted with their sleeping bodies, seems a unique problem; but, for the underde-veloped countries at least, it may very well represent the City of the Future.

How to Cause an Explosion

> I've been in Mongolian villages where people can remember syph-ilis epidemics when, of 2,000 fami-lies, only one baby survived. Now syphilis is eradicated.
>
> —EDGAR SNOW[4]

Ironically, this threatening bulge of population has come about because man has recently been so successful in his age-old battle with nature. In the past, "natural" deaths have always ap-proximately equaled births. Famines and devastating epidemics have often claimed hundreds of thousands of lives at a stroke, and the non-epidemic diseases were, in the long run, even more destructive. "Against the plague," Boccaccio wrote,

all human wisdom and foresight were vain. . . . No doctor's advice, no medicine could overcome or alleviate this disease. . . . Either the disease was such that no treatment was possible or the doctors were so ignorant that they did not know what caused it, and consequently could not administer the proper remedy. In any case, very few re-covered . . .[5]

Now, with remarkable suddenness, all that has been changed. People still starve all too often, but famine relief has become more systematic and efficient. People still die of "unneces-sary" diseases, but governments all over the world, armed with new insecticides, drugs, and vaccines, have undertaken the mass control of disease. The U.N. World Health Organization has in-troduced a dramatic concept of public health, resolving to *eradi-cate* diseases—to cause them simply to pass out of existence. Vast campaigns have scored spectacular gains against malaria, small-pox, cholera, yellow fever, typhus—all the old mass killers. In Ceylon, for instance, deaths from malaria were reduced almost by half in three years. Cholera now exists only in parts of Asia; deaths from cholera were reduced from 130,000 in 1950 to 12,800 in 1960. There has not been a major pandemic, a U.N. publica-tion reports, since 1919, when influenza caused 25 million deaths around the world.[6] Man has seemed to be conquering nature.

But nature is a tricky opponent. It had been keeping a kind of balance, a tragic balance, between births and deaths. The potential of human reproduction is tremendous. In 1798 Thomas Malthus, an English parson-economist, first brought serious at-tention to the now familiar predicament: population tends to increase faster than the means of subsistence. Under good health conditions it is possible for the human race to multiply itself sixty times in less than a century. Nature (among other things) has never yet let this happen; but nature, as we have seen, has recently been deprived of some of its power to destroy, and population is therefore increasing explosively. The world now has one million more mouths to feed every week.

"Overpopulation" is not an easy word to define, because it is relative to economic and social conditions in a given society. But some illustrations will help. For instance:

It took mankind the whole period of recorded time until the early nineteenth century to achieve a population of *one* billion. It took only a century to add the *second* billion. It took somewhat over 30 years to raise the world population to *three* billion. And, at the present rate of increase, only 15 years will be required to bring the figure to *four* billion.[7]

Not only is world population growing, but the *rate* of population growth keeps going up. Over the last eighty years, the rate of *doubling* has doubled.[8]

To put it another way: in 1900, world population increased by about 40,000 people every day; now it is increasing by 180,000 every day. And the rate is going up.

To put it another way: the world is now *adding* to its population about 125 people every minute, 7,500 every hour, more than a million every week, 65 million every year. And the rate is going up.

Overpopulation occurs whenever there are so many people or such a rapid growth of people that the skills and resources of a given area cannot provide them a decent standard. of living.[9] It is a biological form of living beyond one's means. This condition has already been reached in many of the underdeveloped countries. We sometimes hear people discussing World War I "as if it were yesterday"; but world population will probably double before the year 2000, which is not as far in the future as World War I is in the past. By then conditions in the underdeveloped countries will almost certainly be worse, not better, than they are now. And whereas two-thirds of the world's people lived in the underdeveloped countries in 1950, three-quarters of them will be there in the year 2000.

Population, we need to be constantly and forcefully reminded, means people: human beings, who will be hungry if they are not fed, cold if they are not clothed, wretched if they are not housed, and mentally stunted if they are not educated. Yet, of the millions of babies being born into our world this year, most will be ill-fed, ill-clothed, ill-housed, and ill-educated. The world offers them more frustration than fulfillment, more pain than pleasure. This is not prophecy but a present fact.

How Does Hunger Feel?

> Hunger is a curious thing: at first
> it is with you all the time, waking
> and sleeping and in your dreams,
> and your belly cries out insistently,
> and there is a gnawing and a pain
> as if your very vitals were being
> devoured, and you must stop it at
> any cost . . . Then the pain is no
> longer sharp but dull, and this too
> is with you always . . .
> —KAMALA MARKANDAYA[10]

The majority of the world's people are inadequately fed.
In Hong Kong, lean Chinese women with nervous, taut-skinned
faces (their children strapped to their backs and clinging to their
hands) stand in block-long lines waiting for American surplus
food. In the agricultural villages of India (where 80 per cent of
that country's people live), the fields are worn out from centuries
of use and misuse, and subdivided among unnumbered succes-
sions of male heirs until many of them are so small it would be
uneconomical to work them with large modern machinery, even
if it were available. Instead, skinny gray humped oxen endlessly
circle ancient wells in an inefficient attempt to irrigate the crops,
or pull wooden plows, scratching out shallow furrows in the
earth. Manure that should fertilize the soil is burnt for fuel. So
it is not surprising to notice people's lethargy—an inertia born
of hunger and reinforced by generations of fatalistic acceptance
of a system that has never yielded them much except disappointment.

How does it feel to be constantly hungry? Few of us in the
land of the supermarket really know. In the 1940's, Ancel Keys
and his colleagues at the University of Minnesota carried out
an important experiment in semi-starvation. One of the subjects
reported:

I'm hungry. I'm always hungry—not like the hunger that comes when you miss lunch, but a continual cry from the body for food. At times I can almost forget about it but there is nothing that can hold my interest for long. . . . I'm cold. In July I walk downtown on a sunny day with a shirt and sweater on to keep me warm. . . . I'm weak. . . . I trip on cracks in the sidewalk. To open a heavy door it is necessary to brace myself and push or pull with all my might. . . . When I tried to smile it was a grimace and I didn't feel like smiling and never laughed.[11]

The American journalist Dickey Chapelle was once imprisoned by Hungarian Communists as a spy and put on a severely limited diet for an indefinite period. Later she wrote:

Within ten days on this diet I learned something about hunger I had never known . . . It was a local pain as big as my hand, sharp or dull but never still. More important, under the impact of hunger, I watched myself become another person. . . . There was just one mood of which I was capable. Sullen and terrible ugliness. After a time, I thought I probably had forgotten how to weep or curse. I knew I could not laugh.[12]

The fortunate *one-third* of the world's people who do have enough to eat are consuming *two-thirds* of the world's total food production. That is why Americans, members of the lucky one-third, rarely have to experience the pain and lassitude that many of the world's people suffer constantly, and why we can hardly grasp the importance of Gandhi's remark that to a hungry people the only form God dare appear in is the form of food.

The problem of food shortage is closely linked to the problem of bad health. With Western help, American surplus food, and improved transportation, the devastating famines of a few decades ago are currently being thwarted, but although fewer people are actually starving to death, the health of millions is nevertheless still being impaired. In Turkey, for instance, there is now little outright starvation, but people's health suffers because most of them are on a "bread, rice, and beans" diet. When all food is in chronically short supply, as it often is in the underdeveloped countries, the quality of the diet is inevitably low. Foods rich in vitamins are generally expensive, beyond the reach of the great masses of people. The Asian staple of polished rice is also deficient in fat, protein, and minerals; most Asians, Africans, and Latin Americans get far too little meat, fish, and eggs, too little milk, and too few fruits and vegetables to maintain good health.

It is not only that the people cannot afford better foods; in most of the underdeveloped countries these foods simply do not exist in anything like sufficient quantities to supply their expanding populations. Thus, ironically, the eradication of the contagious diseases has tended to increase the diseases of malnutrition; I noticed the symptoms of these everywhere—eyes inflamed with trachoma, bones bent from rickets, thin bodies exhausted from anemia, beriberi, and pellagra. Sickly, tired people do not work well, so the production of food suffers—and a vicious circle is created.

Houses, Schools, Morals

> Say, for instance, that a proud new housing project is begun in a crowded area. All too often by the time the buildings are completed, so many people have moved into, or so many babies have been born into, the area that the number living in poorer, overcrowded homes remains the same.
> —REPORT ON LATIN AMERICA[13]

Another problem caused by explosively growing populations is the shortage of proper housing. Hong Kong, for instance, has jumped from a million and a half to more than three million since World War II. Some of the growth was caused by an influx of refugees from the mainland, but a million babies have also been born in the city in the last fifteen years. Whole families live in little sampans and in makeshift shacks. Some of the lucky ones will eventually move into the comparative luxury of government resettlement buildings—but even there families of seven live in the standard cubicles, about ten feet square.

The situation is little better in many other cities and villages. Two hundred and fifty new families move into Bangkok every day, causing further complications in a country where the national population will double in the next twenty years. This overcrowding of urban areas is going on in most of the underdeveloped countries, with unhappy results. In Indian cities such as Bombay and Calcutta, about one-half of the families live in housing that amounts to one room or less.

Under such conditions, the problem of ill health takes a new form. In Bangkok, people bathe in and drink from the same canals that serve them as open sewers. Bangkok is a city of water and is sometimes called the Venice of the East, but its back streets—where houses are built directly over little ditches used for the disposal of garbage and sewage—are as ugly as anything in the world. In other cities, lack of water causes trouble: half the city dwellers in India must carry their water from ponds and reservoirs, and people who have to carry heavy water jars for many blocks simply cannot use it in great quantities for general cleanliness. Also, cities trying to supply more and more water to exploding populations cannot always manage to assure its purity. Over these crowded masses, therefore, hovers the constant threat of tuberculosis.

If the population explosion continues, it will not be easy—perhaps not even possible—to improve these conditions significantly. An Indian economic expert estimated in 1963 that to give Indians barely adequate housing, twice as much money would be required as is contemplated for all investment in the country's whole economy in the current economic plan.[14] Because of rapid population growth, low-cost housing never keeps up with demand. For example, a recent Inter-American Development Bank loan of one million dollars to the capital of Honduras will supply houses for 4,300 people. But the city is growing by 6,000 people *each year*. This same dismal mathematics is in force throughout the underdeveloped world.

Throughout Asia, the hope of rising from misery is closely linked with the magic of education. From peasants in muddy villages to executives in the centers of government, I found an enthusiasm for education perhaps greater than our own. Yet this simply presents another problem, for less than half the children of these countries are in school.

In Hong Kong it is only one-fourth of the children. The Executive Secretary of the Hong Kong Teacher's Association was deeply concerned. "We cannot keep up with them," he told me. "We have the teachers working in shifts, and the government is constantly building classrooms—but there is another baby born here every four minutes." Furthermore, he said that the school-work of the lucky ones who get into the classroom often suffers because the children are undernourished. And the quality of the instruction suffers even more. In the cities and villages of Asia, great crowds of children sit on the ground around their teachers and recite, at the tops of their voices, their rote lessons; in Bang-kok, university professors have to waste class time reading home-work aloud from textbooks that the students can't afford to buy. Unsatisfactory as all this is, at least these students are better off than the majority of Asian children, who wander about the streets with still smaller children strapped to their backs, and whose minds and lives will always be stunted by illiteracy. The story is the same in all of the underdeveloped countries; only the per-centages vary. Brazil quadrupled its schools between 1933 and 1959, but still only half the children between the ages of seven and fourteen are in school there. In Venezuela, despite heavy investment in school facilities, the national literacy level has dropped from 57 per cent to 51 per cent since World War II.[15] Education is legally compulsory in Thailand, in India, in Egypt, and in Turkey, but in none of these places can this law be en-forced, because exploding populations have created such masses of children that there are neither teachers nor classrooms enough to go around.

One of the most sinister problems connected with rapid population growth is a crisis in morals. There is an ancient Chinese saying: "It is difficult to tell the difference between right and wrong when the stomach is empty." People driven by con-stant hunger, by joblessness, by insecurity; huddled together in overcrowded cities and villages; unaided by education; and with nowhere to turn in their misery—can such people honestly be expected to develop respect for the ethical niceties which admonish them not to covet, not to steal, not even to envy? In poverty-stricken, underdeveloped Sicily, one group of outlaws is known to have spent, collectively, seven hundred and fifty years in school—and more than three thousand years in prison.[16] While I was in New Delhi, Tara Ali Baig, General Secretary of the Indian Council for Child Welfare, wrote about the slum dwellers of Delhi in the *Hindustan Times*:

They live in tiny sheds made from flattened oil tins and gunny sacking. Almost any slum scene is that of a woman with two or three tiny immobile children squatting beside her while she feeds the one in her arms . . . Desperation and insecurity become, for a family like this, a second nature, blighting their entire lives.[17]

This "blight" is both physical and moral, and it will doubtless spread right along with the growth of the misery-ridden people.

This suggests another, subtler moral problem, and one that concerns us all directly: the present growth of world population may seem so overwhelming, so inevitable, as to cause us, the comparatively well-to-do peoples of the world, simply to throw up our hands—to disclaim responsibility for helping those less well off than we. That is a particularly tempting corruption, simply because it is so easy, and seems so "sensible." Repelled as I was by the first sight of Asian misery, I could not help remarking on the psychological defense mechanism that gradually dulled my shock at the sight of old women carrying heavy loads on bamboo poles through the streets of Hong Kong, or that somehow permitted visiting Americans to lie comfortably in the over-staffed luxury of the Grand Hotel of Calcutta, while outside thousands of half-starved human beings were sleeping in the streets under thin rags. Everyone who has lived in Asia knows why this defense mechanism operates: it is the only way the mind can keep its sanity in an insane situation. It does not always work perfectly; I saw one well-to-do Indian who, when accosted by a beggar, lectured him severely—and then burst into tears. Personal compassion notwithstanding, however, the basic, unhappy situation remains, and it is now a familiar story: overpopulation reinforces poverty, poverty generates desperation,

and desperation leads to immorality. It is perhaps worth reminding ourselves that the immorality of the envious poor who rebel
against their painful lot is no worse than the immorality of the
comfortable rich who too easily accept such intolerable
conditions.

What Can Be Done?

> So long as we are concerned with
> the quality of life, we have no
> choice but to be concerned with
> the quantity of life.
> —RICHARD N. GARDNER[18]

The problems of the underdeveloped, overpopulated countries are extremely difficult ones. What can be done about them?
Loans and gifts from the wealthier countries are, for the time
being, essential; but they are only a stopgap. A proper solution
must begin by creating more food—not in the nations that already have enough, but in those where people desperately need
it. Ambitious moves are being made in this direction. In India,
in Egypt, in Turkey, and elsewhere, irrigation is being extended,
production of fertilizer is being stepped up, acreage is being increased, and better crop plants are being produced. But in
many of the underdeveloped countries, domestic food supplies
are nevertheless still falling behind population growth. A gigantic
agricultural effort will be necessary simply to keep greater and
greater numbers of people in their present malnourished condition.

Industrial development in the underdeveloped countries is
also imperative, and attempts are being made to build strong
local industries. But industrial growth depends upon capital investment, and capital is scarce in these needy areas. Furthermore,
merely to keep per capita incomes at their present low levels
through the next few decades, huge annual investments—from

6 to 10 per cent of national incomes—will be necessary. To permit a noticeable and encouraging growth in per capita incomes, investment would have to reach 12 or 15 per cent or more—rates that are not likely to materialize in the underdeveloped areas. Thus, in industrial production as well as in food production, the future looks dim indeed: instead of relieving people's misery, enormous and well-intentioned agricultural and industrial efforts may end up simply maintaining more people in greater misery. Rapid population growth is saying to the underdeveloped economies, in effect, what the Red Queen said to Alice: "It takes all the running *you* can do to keep in the same place. If you want to get somewhere else, you must run at least twice as fast as that!"

Then what *is* to be done? I asked the question everywhere in Asia. There were no easy answers, but I often heard the rather wistful remark: "If only the population were not growing so fast!" And, just as often: "Medical science has lowered our death rate; if only it would help to lower our birth rate!" This was not an attempt to reduce all problems to a matter of birth control, but a realization that without regulation of births, the other problems are insoluble.

Some effort is already being made in the underdeveloped countries to encourage limitation of births. The governments of India, Pakistan, Egypt, Ceylon, South Korea, and other countries are officially sponsoring family planning programs. Unfortunately, though, none of these has yet reached far enough into the villages to have had a significant effect on national growth rates.

One drawback to such programs is that peasant peoples are generally motivated to want more, not fewer, children. This is partly because of the age-old approval of fertility as such. For example, in Benares I once saw women tying rocks to temple trees in the pious belief that this would bring more sons; in Greece, according to Margaret Mead, childlessness is considered a "terrible calamity";[19] in Latin America, newlywed husbands feel they must produce children quickly to prove they are "real men"; and in Mexico, writes one scholar, "a large family is . . . the supreme cultural and religious value . . . mothers are surrounded by an emotional veneration second only to that of the Virgin

Mother herself."[20] Partly, too, large families are a kind of substitute for social security. Few of the underdeveloped countries
have, or are planning to have soon, a social security system, and
a large number of sons seems the only protection against the
hazards of old age.

Among upper-class people in the cities, these ideas are beginning to disappear. I was in New Delhi on India's national
Family Planning Day in 1960. A considerable amount of ex-
citement seemed to have been generated: debates, displays, newspaper articles, and so on. But most of this interest, I was told by
Lt. Col. B. L. Raina, Director of Family Planning for the Indian
Government, is limited to the cities, where it is least needed.
Massive education, he said, has to be undertaken in the villages,
where the great bulk of the people live. There, many people do
not even know that family size is controllable. Too often, an Indian demographer told me, it is supposed that a propaganda
poster (in English!) will solve the problem; whereas what is
really needed is a large staff of trained and sympathetic people
who will go into the villages and advise the people about family
planning.

"Motivation," then, is an important part of the whole problem of population limitation, and it is a complex one. What sort
of motivation for family limitation is needed, for instance, given
presently available contraceptives? The expense, the relative in-
convenience, and the unreliability of these devices make a high
degree of motivation necessary. Considerably less motivation
would be required if a simpler, cheaper, more reliable contraceptive were available. "What we really need in India today,"
says M. C. Chagla, formerly India's ambassador to the United
States, "is a cheap oral contraceptive."[21] Ayub Khan, the president of Pakistan, calls the rapidly growing population Pakistan's
"Problem Number One" and has asked Americans "to apply your
mind and your resources to be able to combat this problem."[22]
But so far, the simple contraceptive that both these nations need
and want does not exist.

Contraceptive pills are now widely used in some countries.
They are effective and safe under medical supervision, but they
are still too expensive and too complicated to be of any use to
poor, illiterate peasants. (The directions for Enovid, the first of

mated. Egypt's last census also revealed "extra" millions. So did Pakistan's. So did Brazil's and Ghana's and Mexico's and Venezuela's and those of other countries as well. Where population statistics are not wholly reliable, then, it seems prudent to assume that the situation is worse, not better, than it is estimated to be; when dealing with unknown quantities, we should deal with probabilities, not wishful thoughts.

Tranquilizer No. 3: The Migration Mirage

"If some countries, like China or India, seem to have too many people, why not let them move to countries like Australia or Canada, that have too few?"

"Let them emigrate" is a temptingly simple formula, but, like that other facile solution, "Let them eat cake," it is simply not practical.

In the first place, emigration will not work because on the whole people do not like to uproot themselves. Spectacular natural disasters, such as the Irish potato famine in the nineteenth century, can force large numbers of people to move to foreign lands, but ordinarily people prefer to stay at home, however humble. Even as mobile a person as the American small farmer, currently driven off the land in increasing numbers by the competition of corporate farms, usually feels a wrench at moving just a few miles and undertaking a new life for which he is not well prepared. This natural reluctance has to be multiplied many times to approximate the suspicions and fears that emigration to foreign lands would cause a traditional peasant, living in the same village his forefathers had lived in, tilling the same fields, planting the same crops with the same implements, worshipping the same local deities, talking the same dialect and practicing the same habits as the neighbors with whom he and his relatives have "always" socialized, cooperated, and intermarried. On the island of Java, for instance, the Dutch, like the other colonial Powers after World War II, helped to wipe out diseases; as a result, Java now suffers from severe population pressures. Other nearby islands, notably Sumatra, are less thickly populated, but it is almost impossible to persuade the Javanese to move even the comparatively few miles to these islands.

In the second place, emigration will not work because there are few habitable, underpopulated areas left. Large numbers of people cannot sustain themselves in deserts or swamps, on glaciers or mountaintops. Enormous stretches of the earth's surface are thus unavailable to man. Only with tremendous investment of money and labor can humans extend habitable areas farther up the sides of mountains or into deserts or the sea, and such investment is hard to come by. Asians sometimes mention the "vast" and sparsely-settled island continent of Australia as an area available for emigration. But Australia's size is illusory. Only 7.5 per cent of that land mass seems likely ever to be brought into cultivation, and much of that only by tremendous expenditures of capital.[3] Australia might be able to absorb fifteen million more people.[4] But (a) this amounts to only one year's increase in China alone, and (b) Australia's own population (now about eleven million) is growing so fast that it will probably double in about thirty years; the Australians apparently need no outside help in filling up whatever open spaces they can afford to make livable.

Finally, emigration will not work because most nations, with their restrictive immigration quotas, will not permit it. When tens of thousands of Chinese poured out of Red China into Hong Kong in 1962, the United States was willing to accept only five thousand. The British, who have been working diligently to provide places for Chinese refugees, on this occasion alone had to turn back fifty thousand people. But to accommodate the growth of Asian populations by emigration, the world would be asked to find room not for thousands or tens of thousands, but for *hundreds of millions*. For purposes of comparison, remember that the United States received from Europe fewer than thirty-five million immigrants during the last century. That is less than one year's population growth in Asia.

Tranquilizer No. 4: The "Automatic" Fallacy

"Higher living standards will automatically lower birth rates; this is known as the 'demographic transition.' It happened this way in Europe and the United States—why not in Asia?"

It would be pleasant to think, as (according to a 1963 Gallup Poll) many Americans apparently do, that "nature will take care of things somehow"—that there is some beneficent mechanism that is now raising living standards, whereupon, like an obliging Rube Goldberg contraption, birth rates will subside, thus causing even greater rises in living standards, and so on. Unfortunately, the standard of living is *not* rising significantly in the underdeveloped countries. During the last ten years, India has managed to expand its Gross National Product by only *one dollar* per person per year.[5] Those hungry, hollow-eyed men, women, and children are not a thing of the past; they are with us today, and they (more and more of them) will be with us tomorrow, and the next day—still hungry, still sickly, still waiting for the chance to be something more than neglected animals.

"But surely, all that American economic assistance . . ."

Economic aid from the developed nations to the under-developed ones is a minimal necessity for well-being in our world. But although it is a necessity, it is not in itself sufficient. Two decades ago, as a seaman in the Merchant Marine, I first saw the crumbling houses, the dirt and decay of an underdeveloped country in Latin America. I was shocked at the poverty there; but what is more significant, some of my Latin American shipmates who had not recently seen their home were also dismayed. The place, they insisted, had got worse, not better.

That was in 1946. Since that time various forms of United States aid have been sent to Latin America. The Alliance for

Progress proudly reported in 1963 that its programs have resulted in the construction of "an estimated 140,000 low and middle-income homes" in the first two years of its existence.[6] But in the same two years, the population of Latin America grew by about *ten million* people, and (again according to Alliance for Progress figures) about 40 per cent of the population do not have minimally adequate housing. The foreign aid money has done some good, but it has not been sufficient to cope with the population explosion.

"But what about the 'demographic transition'? Haven't populations always leveled off as nations became more urbanized?"

Not always: the United States and the Soviet Union, for instance, are now growing at very rapid rates. A demographic transition did occur in many developing nations in the nineteenth century, but it is not an automatic mechanism, and there is good reason to think that it cannot be repeated in the same way in the currently underdeveloped countries.[7] Furthermore, this transition, when it does occur, characteristically begins with a temporary acceleration of numbers, and this acceleration might well be severe enough, in underdeveloped countries, to frustrate all development strategies.

Moreover, recent studies indicate that urbanization not only fails to lower fertility in underdeveloped countries, but even tends to stimulate it. Asian peasants, by sheer weight of numbers, are now being forced off their inadequate lands and into nearby cities. (From 20 to 40 per cent of the people in many Asian cities are now squatters—former peasants who have simply moved in and found an empty place to build a shack.) But these cities are not as industrialized as Western ones, and so the peasants, once there, do not become "citified," but instead create colonies resembling their old village societies. The Asian city, then, becomes largely an enormous, poverty-ridden cluster of villages. The people there are often no more knowledgeable, no more rational, no more sophisticated, no more cosmopolitan than they were before they moved. Their fertility remains high, and sometimes even gets higher.[8]

"*But if Japan was able to reduce its rate of population growth, why can't other countries?*"

Unfortunately, Japan cannot serve as a model for the rest of Asia. Its industrialization began more than three-quarters of a century ago and proceeded during a time of comparatively low population growth. During the same three-quarters of a century, the nation made itself almost totally literate. Also, more than any other Asian people, the Japanese live in industrialized, modernized cities. With these powerful advantages, Japan was able to recognize its population problem and, largely by legal abortions, to revolutionize its birth rate in less than fifteen years. But no other Asian (or any underdeveloped) country has these advantages—and therefore no such country is likely to repeat Japan's experience.

Tranquilizer No. 5: Science Fiction

"*In this age of scientific achievement, we can overcome any difficulties caused by population growth. If necessary, we could find new sources of food and migrate to other planets.*"

We have come to expect great things from the laboratories, but we had better not stretch our luck. The population explosion is happening right now, and will get worse every year. Meanwhile the United States, with its best efforts and after many embarrassing delays, has succeeded in putting only a few men briefly into orbit. To talk about our fledgling space instruments as a means of solving a *current* problem is not only absurd; it is irresponsible. To think of space vehicles as solving future problems is hardly more reassuring. Presumably none of us would be delighted at the prospect of living on Venus, for instance, in temperatures hundreds of degrees above boiling, or on the moon, in temperatures hundreds of degrees below zero.

What about reaching other solar systems, where some hypothetical planet might be more hospitable? This is how one scientist describes the possibilities:

> Assuming that the world could support a population of 10 billion and that population growth continues at the present rate, in 70 years it would be necessary to move 170 million people each year. Assuming 100 passengers per spaceship, the migration would require 1.7 million spaceships each year—at a cost . . . of $300 million per ship. But if birth control is not to be practiced on earth, it would surely not be practiced on the spaceships. If only one couple started the trip, the number of progeny (even allowing for the deleterious effects of inbreeding) would be about 2000 at the end of the trip. Thus it would be necessary to provide 85 million spaceships every year, each with a capacity of 2000 and at a cost of several billion dollars or more per ship.[9]

In short, scientific panaceas—the attractive visions of widespread solar and atomic power, civilian space travel, plentiful and palatable food from new sources, and so on—are still too far in the future to be practicably relevant to the present population problem. It is no help to people who are hungry *now* to advise them that "We'll fix everything tomorrow." I do not mean to foreclose on the future; scientists may yet have some quick and pleasant surprises in store. New plant strains, new pesticides and fertilizers, and better animal husbandry will almost certainly improve agricultural prospects; furthermore, British scientists have reportedly had some success in creating milk directly from green plants; an M.I.T. nutritionist has developed a powder from cottonseed, corn, and sorghum that is nutritionally comparable to milk; American chemists are testing an entirely synthetic diet; cheap and available soybean extracts and fish flour are both high in proteins; protein may even be produced from petroleum; and the sea can be made to supply more food than it has yet yielded. All such developments are more than welcome, but encouraging as they are, they have not yet solved the problem of nourishing the world's expanding population, nor do they seem likely to do so in the near future. In the meantime, we must continue to deal with realities and probabilities, not with science fiction.

Tranquilizer No. 6: The Loaves-and-Fishes Theory of Agriculture

"Let's stop worrying about population and start thinking about production. Better agriculture can provide food for any foreseeable population."

Certainly more food must be produced. Most of the world's people are malnourished now, and with 65 million more mouths at the world's dinner table annually, the crop equivalent of about 65 million new acres is needed each year, simply to keep the world's people at their current, malnourished level. B. R. Sen, Director General of the U.N. Food and Agriculture Organization, warned in 1963 that improving nutrition throughout the world would require a doubling of world food production by 1980 and a fourfold increase by the year 2000.[10] But at the same time he also reported that the gap between food supplies of the "rich" nations and those of the "poor" nations was widening.

Can new farmland and new agricultural techniques keep pace with the increasing demand? Past experience has often been discouraging. In 1952 Charles Galton Darwin described one major project in what is now Pakistan:

Not long ago the province of Sind was mainly desert; the ground was quite fertile but there was no rainfall. A great engineering undertaking, the Sukkur barrage, has spread the waters of the Indus over a very wide area, and turned much of the desert into a garden. According to the universally accepted standards this was a great benefit to the world, for it made possible the adequate feeding of a people previously on the verge of starvation. But things did not work out like that, for after a few years the effect was only to have a large number of people on the verge of starvation instead of a small number.[11]

Thus four thousand square miles of the earth's surface were brought into cultivation—and fully settled in one generation, while the density of population in the rest of the country increased.

Egypt is having a similar experience with the Aswan high dam. The rapid expansion of Egypt's population makes it already certain that the spectacular project will be able at best only to check temporarily the falling standard of living in Egypt. For while the high dam may increase agricultural production in Egypt by as much as 45 per cent, Egypt's population will have risen by about that same figure during the time the dam is being built, leaving Egypt with the same problem it had, but on a larger scale.[12] In the underdeveloped countries, Malthus' grim mathematics keeps asserting itself.

While it is possible—in fact, imperative—to make greater efforts to produce more food, the Cornucopians sometimes give the impression that past and present efforts in this direction have been negligible and that therefore any future efforts at all are sure to meet with great success. On the contrary, in many places in Asia an astonishingly thorough use is now being made of the earth. In Formosa, for instance, the mountainsides have been painstakingly terraced high up, in a series of gradations, the farmers growing rice, tea, or vegetables on the lower slopes and bamboo and acacia on the higher, steeper slopes. A Formosan commission for rural development is preparing hundreds of thousands of acres of these hillsides, reclaiming tens of thousands of acres of tidelands, amalgamating farms to eliminate waste, building roads and irrigation canals, improving fertilizers, seeds, and pesticides, and encouraging two, three, or more crops per year, as well as "intercropping" and "relay planting" (ingenious ways of making the soil produce more than one crop at a time). But Formosa has one of the highest rates of population growth in the world, and, despite all this agricultural activity, has not managed to remain self-sufficient in food production. Formosa now imports more food than it exports.

Similarly, other nations make better use of the sea as a source of food than we do. I became very fond of Japanese seaweed products—of which there are dozens, ranging from something like hard cookies and popcorn to the tasty, pliable wrappings around their raw fish delicacies. Indeed, the Japanese, unlike us squeamish Americans, seem to eat almost anything that grows, swims, or crawls in the water.

There are no doubt better ways of farming the sea than even the Orientals have yet discovered, and some experts think it possible to double present marine production. Cultivating, fertilizing, and transplanting are all concepts which may eventually be more fruitful in sea farming than they now are. But the limitations are also real. Fish production is grossly inefficient. Livestock on land is almost entirely plant-fed, but fish suitable for canning are all carnivores which have fed on other carnivores or on herbivores. Thus most of our seafood is the result of a very inefficient chain of production: to convert food from plants to herbivores to carnivores involves a loss of 99 per cent of the original plant food value. The harvesting of seafoods has its own problems. The danger of over-fishing to the point of the extinction or near-extinction of some species is already serious, as the decline of formerly thriving canneries in many areas testifies.[13]

But even assuming that the land and the sea could be better used, assuming that the whole world's peasant population could emulate the dogged determination of certain Indian farmers who till land so high up on the Himalayas that they have to carry soil up to their rocky terraces in baskets (and replace it after the spring rains), the question would still remain: ought people to extend cultivation to all parts of the earth? Are there good reasons for not trying to farm some areas?

Certainly excessive zeal can cause errors of every degree of seriousness. In Burma, European agricultural experts introduced deep plowing—and in doing so, broke up the hardpan that held the water in the rice paddies. They encouraged weeding the rubber plantations—and thereby reduced the production of sap. In Greece, fertilizing the fields caused wheat to be less resistant to drought.[14]

But the results can be even worse. Remember again the deserts now shifting over Persepolis, over Petra, over Libya. When men cultivate lands that ecologically ought not to be cultivated, or when they overcultivate them or cultivate them badly, it is all too easy for erosion to turn them into dust bowls. The distinguished Belgian botanist Raymond Bouillenne writes of his studies in Africa:

Cultivation is abandoned when the soil becomes unproductive. Then herbaceous plants appear and are generally used as pasture. Because of the need for pastureland, grassland has been burnt off so that it will not become wooded. Where this is done, a great number of useful plants disappear, to be replaced by a small number of pyrophilous varieties that are often not suitable even for pasture. The vegetative cover disintegrates, especially when, as often happens, there is overgrazing. The soil, laid bare, undergoes extensive changes in structure and composition. It loses its colloids, becomes dust, hardens into laterite, or is carried away by erosion. . . . In the Congo agronomists have shown that in 6 years 30,000 square kilometers of soil have been ruined. In Madagascar the drama has been played out over a period of 60 years. This island was once covered with splendid forests; today 70 percent of its area is occupied by an ocean of tough grasses, ravaged by fire and unsuitable even for the feeding of herds. In short, *we are in the throes of an apparently irreversible progressive reduction of the surface of cultivable lands. It is estimated that the area of such lands on the earth has decreased by 20 percent in the last hundred years. Of the 40 billion acres remaining today, at least 20 million disappear irretrievably each year.*[15]

The grandeur that hovers over the ruins of past civilizations is a tragic grandeur. Man has found it possible to change the face of the earth, but the change has all too often been—and to an unfortunate extent continues to be—destructive; in the end, mankind has found it self-destructive. Thus one of the most melancholy aspects of the population explosion is that it not only torments people now with hunger, disease, and all kinds of hardships, but also harshly threatens the next generation, and the next, and the next.

The loaves-and-fishes agricultural theorists will nevertheless insist that more food "could" be produced. And of course it will have to be, if mass starvation is to be avoided. But will it be enough, and soon enough?

Through four nations of Southeast Asia runs the world's tenth largest river, the Mekong. Until recently, virtually nothing had been done by way of developing it: it produced no electricity at all, and only 3 per cent of the surrounding land was irrigated.

Now the United Nations Economic Commission for Asia and the Far East (ECAFE) has undertaken the development of the lower Mekong valley. With irrigation, much now useless land could produce two or three crops of rice annually, with high yields; diversification of crops should also be possible. Flood control, navigation, and electrification should be stimulated. This project could change the face of much of Southeast Asia; it could be a pattern for the future.

But lest anyone snap his fingers and proclaim the battle won, consider this. Work cannot begin on dam-building until extensive and accurate engineering investigations are carried out: on elevations, on hydrology, on the effect of tributaries on the main stream. This work must almost always be done from scratch in underdeveloped countries. It is expensive: investigative engineering work on the Mekong project used one-third of the total funds—thirty million dollars—that the United Nations then had available for *all* world development. It is time-consuming: proper hydrological measurements require more than thirty years; a risky minimum is five years. When these preliminaries are finished, final engineering designs require approximately two more years; financing adds a year; *then* building can begin. Building major dams requires at least six years. The problems of land reform, canal-building, and re-education of peasants can be attacked concurrently, but they are almost certain to delay the final development.

Thus a bare minimum of about fifteen years intervenes between the idea and the beginning of productive use of such projects. But what happens to the population in the meantime? Thailand recently took a census and the government was shocked to discover that the nation is growing by more than 3 per cent per year; that is, it will double its numbers in less than twenty-three years. The Malthusian specter reappears: even with this bold international plan, the future is still uncertain in Southeast Asia.

A critical lack of time, then, is a major obstacle to the success of such development projects. But lack of money is equally threatening. The cost of the Mekong development will be about ten billion dollars. Fourteen nations and eleven United Nations agencies are cooperating to bear this cost. Presumably the economic benefits of the project will eventually be greater than the expenditures. Still, how many such projects will available world development funds support? How many are geographically promising? How many will be required to keep up with current population growth? It costs about fifty dollars to bring an acre of new land into high productivity.[16] That means something like seven million dollars a day just to keep up with current population increase in the underdeveloped countries. That figure has to be kept in mind whenever the loaves-and-fishes agriculturists talk about what "could" be accomplished.

A simpler approach would be to intensify yields on presently cultivated land. Some F.A.O. experts think that current yields could be raised by half—in some cases even doubled—by more intensive use of fertilizers, manures, and legumes.[17] But the image this may present to Westerners—of a well-to-do farmer driving his tractor and wagon loaded with chemical fertilizers across a broad, deeply plowed field—is of course misleading. The peasants of underdeveloped societies are not going to be able to use such fertilizers unless they are produced in much greater quantities, and marketed at a price the peasants can afford to pay. Furthermore, the peasants must, in most countries, be taught how to use them—which means training large numbers of technicians who must be able and willing to spend their lives in the countryside, tactfully and patiently demonstrating the advantages of these new and alien products.

Also, once again, there is the stumbling block of expense. Intensifying farming by better fertilization does not mean a sort of salt-shaker sprinkling of cheap chemicals on a hitherto barren earth which then will spring magically into bloom. Bringing an old, worn-out field into high productivity requires considerable investment in labor and materials—about twenty dollars per acre, according to the noted geochemist Harrison Brown, who estimates that to double world food production by a combination of intensifying and extending farming would cost about 100 billion dollars.[18] Where is that much money to come from? (Remember that the average per capita income in many underdeveloped countries is less than one hundred dollars per year.) The fact is that despite the claims of the loaves-and-fishes school that food supplies "could" be doubled, *no one*—

from private citizen to national or international organization—
is planning practical action on a large enough scale to do it.

Even if these tremendous sums of money were available,
however, other problems would be certain to delay agricultural
development. Too often, markets are unreliable; prices fluctuate;
transport, handling, and storage facilities are inadequate; sources
of fertilizers and other materials are limited; and the farmer's
incentive is therefore undermined.

Moreover, underdeveloped societies are often not progressive and idealistic about their development, but feudalistic and
corrupt. I once heard Prime Minister Nehru proudly describe
his government's protracted legal struggles to achieve land
reform in India, where large tracts had been in the hands of
wealthy and socially irresponsible landowners. Even there, however, the struggle for land reform has not yet been won, and in
many of the underdeveloped countries it has not even begun.

And there is the traditional conservatism of the peasant.
India's peasants, Nehru said, are "very much in a rut about
everything . . . running the farms as people used to farm a
hundred, two hundred, five hundred years ago, hardly any
change." Once you have seen the listless women squatting to
cut grain with a little sickle, or the men driving skinny oxen
around a well, slowly irrigating the fields, you realize that
agricultural progress is going to be slow. Consider this true,
albeit incredible, case history. Most villages in underdeveloped
countries do not have a system of running water; water is carried
from wells to the homes. Sometimes the closest well is at some
distance from the village itself. In one such village in India a
government worker recently tried to persuade the villagers to
have water piped into the village. This suggestion was received
with deep suspicion, particularly by the village elders, who
pointed out that the women had "always" carried the water from
the well. After two months of alternating persuasion with studied
indifference, the government worker made some headway against
this argument, but then encountered a stiffer one: some villagers
were very much against people of all castes using the same tap.
More months of argument, reinforced by direct appeals to the
women, finally won out. But from the first proposal of this
seemingly obvious benefit until water finally reached the village,

a full year passed. Clearly, new methods of irrigation, fertilization, and farm modernization simply are not going to be thrust upon such people overnight.

Nor will every other apparently reasonable Western plan necessarily work out smoothly in other cultures. The agricultural expert from Iowa, Jonathan Garst, who has many plausible and encouraging things to say about the value of fertilizers, seriously underestimates the cultural problems involved in feeding the world. "People like to eat meat, milk, and eggs," he writes; and "India has more cattle than any other country."[19] But in fact Buddhists do not take easily to drinking milk, and the thought of eating a cow, to the orthodox Hindu, is as repellent as Jonathan Swift's ironic proposal that the Irish eat their babies.

None of this should be taken to imply that underdeveloped countries ought to abandon the task of agricultural development. Quite the contrary: the whole world must make a concerted effort to produce more food—much more food. But to assume that hypothetical future increases in food supplies are at the same level of probability as the present and continuing expansion of population is to ignore the grim realities. For years the loaves-and-fishes agriculturalists have been insisting that underdeveloped countries "could" do better; but in India, since 1960, food production has not increased at all—the only increase has been in the number of hungry people.

Tranquilizer No. 7: The Panacea of Industrialization

"If we want to help the underdeveloped countries, we should help them get started on industrialization. Industries create jobs, produce goods, raise living standards, and supply materials for foreign trade. In short, industrialization will solve the economic problems of the presently underdeveloped countries."

Industrialization is an essential part of economic development, of course. But here again, if we are going to be realistic, serious obstacles must be recognized. The cost must be kept in mind. Creating new industries in the underdeveloped countries is relatively inexpensive—roughly about $1,500 per worker—but calculating at even that modest figure, new industries would cost tens of billions of dollars a year, simply to accommodate the *new* annual entrants into the labor force. No one has yet suggested a realistic source for this much investment capital. Individual savings are not likely to provide it in countries where annual per capita income is less than one hundred dollars, and normal foreign investments tend to gravitate toward the industrialized, not toward the underdeveloped countries, because (1) foreign investors are often skeptical of local management; (2) the uncertain political future of many underdeveloped countries discourages investment; (3) the lack of acknowledged priorities in local development schemes frustrates potential investors; (4) outside economic help (like that of the United States Agency for International Development or the Alliance for Progress) is sometimes viewed with suspicion by legislators in the lending countries and therefore restricted or limited to short-term projects.

Behind this discouraging picture is an even more discouraging basic problem. An industrial society can only operate properly when it is founded on an "infrastructure," not only of natural resources but of schools, roads and railroads, power sources, public health, irrigation, technical knowledge, and skilled labor —all man-made resources which themselves require years of patient and prudent investment and administration. Financing these things is an extremely difficult task. Long-term lending institutions prefer to finance projects which eventually pay off. And infrastructure, though a necessary foundation of an industrial society, never pays off directly.

Indeed, the very act of building this infrastructure in an underdeveloped society is sometimes self-sabotaging. Education, for instance, is an expensive item in the budget of developing countries. It *must* be promoted: an industrial nation needs a broad base of literacy for even semi-skilled labor; it needs a large number of well-educated people to carry on administrative work; and it needs a considerable number of highly trained educators, medical personnel, and technicians. It is not difficult to find volunteers for these roles. But, as I discovered in Egypt, in

Formosa, and elsewhere, many of the educated young people in these countries find ways of emigrating permanently to Europe or the United States; thus their skills (and the cost of their education) are lost to their countries. Even those who remain at home are not always efficiently used, for, quite naturally, young doctors, teachers, and other professional people prefer the comfort and advantages of big cities, where they are less needed, to a Spartan existence in semi-primitive villages, where they are needed very badly.

Finally, the very existence of large numbers of young people creates an enormous strain on investment capital. In many underdeveloped countries, more than half the population is under twenty years of age. Thus education and housing absorb vast amounts of capital that might otherwise be used for industrial investment.

The matter of investment is, of course, crucial. Typically, an underdeveloped country saves and invests only about 5 per cent of its national income. W. W. Rostow writes:

The difference between a traditional and a modern society is merely a question of whether the investment rate is low relative to population increase—let us say under 5% of national income; or whether it has risen up to 10% or over . . .[20]

To reach a point of economic "take-off," Rostow says, an underdeveloped society must not only achieve this difficult rate of investment but at the same time develop a high growth rate in the manufacturing sector and, of course, the political, social, and institutional incentives for such growth. Rapid population growth hampers all of these things.

As a rule of thumb, economists generally assume that it takes about three dollars of investment to produce one dollar of net national product; so, if a nation's population is growing by 2 or 3 per cent (as many are), an investment of from 6 to 9 per cent of net national product is needed simply to *sustain* the current per capita national product. To improve upon this— to raise the per capita national product by even 2 per cent per year—would require an investment of 12 to 15 per cent of the net national product; and the prospect of achieving such an in-

vestment in most underdeveloped countries, given the difficulties
enumerated above, is not at all bright.[21]

To make matters worse, the prospect of industrial progress
in underdeveloped countries is complicated by all sorts of social
and political problems. American businessmen who are not
familiar with these countries tend to think of them in terms of
their own experience and see their expanding populations as
"marketing opportunities" or "new demand" or "booming
growth." They do not seem to realize how little effective demand
there is in a poverty-ridden people. Nor do they distinguish between the healthy dynamism that moderate population increase
can stimulate, and the unhealthy strains that too-rapid population increase causes. Nor do they take into account the semi-
feudal, oligarchic nature of many of these societies; or the intense
and growing nationalism that obstructs trade; or the plaguing
balance-of-payment difficulties, especially in the newly independent states; or the extremely low economic base from which
these countries are starting.

Americans also need to realize how seriously under-employ-
ment affects densely populated countries, even those which are
relatively highly industrialized: Tokyo businesses, for instance,
hire numerous young women simply to serve tea to the productive workers, and Tokyo department stores hire dozens of pretty
girls who do nothing but stand at the tops and bottoms of
escalators, bowing to the passing customers while pretending to
wipe the moving rail. There are probably seven million such
nearly useless "workers" in the Japanese economy.[22] Americans
also need to understand how badly wealth is distributed in many
of these countries. In Benares, in the midst of ragged, hollow-
eyed people, stands an incredible maharaja's palace: huge,
ornate, vulgar, filled with gilded statues, crystal chandeliers, and
the skins of more than three hundred tigers the maharaja has
shot. The day of the maharaja is passing in India, but in most
underdeveloped countries his economic counterpart still exists,
and in strength.

In short, although industrialization would help to solve
some of the economic problems of poor countries, it is highly
unlikely that it will come fast enough to overtake unregulated
population expansion. Historically, it has taken something like

sixty years to move a society from the beginning of economic take-off to maturity. It is improbable that it can be accomplished that fast in the underdeveloped countries. And even sixty more years of unregulated population growth in these countries will almost certainly swamp any conceivable attempt at economic development. Again, this is simply a matter of facing up to probabilities.

Tranquilizer No. 8: Cornucopianism and Conservation

"Overpopulation will not exhaust our raw materials; with our new sources of power and improved extracting methods, we may consider our material supplies to be virtually limitless."

The world's non-renewable resources have lasted as long as they have principally because so few of the world's people have been using them. Americans, who make up only 6 per cent of the world's population, consume one-third of the world's raw material production.[23] The United States uses up eighteen tons of various materials per person per year, much of which is imported. (Eighteen out of twenty-nine principal minerals vital to our economy are now supplied chiefly by imports.) We annually require about half a ton of steel per person, India only about twenty-five pounds.

Aside from the immediate moral question as to whether we have a right to use up these world supplies so voraciously, this raises another, even more far-reaching question: if industrialization does come about in the emerging nations, and the other 94 per cent of the world's multiplying peoples improve their standards of living—as they have every right to—what will happen to the demand for raw materials then? It is instructive to remember that between 1900 and 1950 the population of the United States doubled—but the rising expectations of the American people caused our use of minerals to increase eight times and our use of fuels thirteen times.[24] Engineers, it is true, have displayed remarkable ingenuity in improving extractive processes and finding substitute materials (though, it should be noted, with ever-rising costs); nevertheless, with world population simultaneously expanding and going through a revolution of rising expectations, the non-renewable resources of our planet are going to be subject to an unprecedented and devastating drain.

Intelligence and Alternatives

> New [mental] patients were put in a room with concrete walls and floors, and each was given a large mop. An attendant then would turn on a big faucet and go out, closing the door behind him.
> The insane would go to work with the mops.
> The sane would turn off the tap.
> —WILLIAM VOGT[25]

Since most of us have troubles of our own and are therefore easily attracted to social tranquilizers, we need to be continuously reminding ourselves that the euphemism "underdeveloped" cloaks a desperate cry for help from hungry, sickly people living in mud huts and scrapwood shacks across great stretches of the world; that the population explosion is here and now; and that if it continues, it will doom the poverty-stricken people to even worse conditions. "We are coming to a situation," says Eugene R. Black, President of the World Bank, "in which the optimist will be the man who thinks that present living standards can be maintained. The pessimist will not look even for that."[26]

As a nation we have been, for all practical purposes, ignoring this prospect. We have, it is true, provided for economic assistance to many underdeveloped countries, and such aid is a necessary part of an eventual solution of their problems; but it is only a part, not the whole. What the leaders of government in India and Pakistan have recently and urgently requested of us is something essential and fundamental: a means of limiting population growth so that their economic efforts can have a chance of success. Ambassador Chagla has asked, "If you are willing to give us loans and grants, to give us millions of tons of wheat, why are you not willing to give us the benefit of your scientific and technical knowledge . . . ?" The three billion dollars in past U.S. aid to India, he said, is largely "being nullified by the increase in population."[27]

What the Cornucopians are advocating is a "philosophy-of-could," by which, they claim, "We'll fix everything tomorrow." It would be very pleasant if it became obvious tomorrow that they were right; but so far that has not become obvious. Therefore, if we are going to be practical about the formidable problem of poverty in our time, we must shake off the tranquilizing temptations of the philosophy-of-could and admit frankly that we "can" do only what we actually *do* do. No other definition of our capabilities will serve.

Using such a compellingly honest criterion, we will quickly understand how irresponsible are the hopes of the Cornucopians. For their plans are grounded on the most precarious and improbable assumptions: that serious national and international tensions will not interrupt the progress they so confidently predict; that governments will efficiently use, not misuse, economic assistance; that economic overlords will suddenly begin to act in the interest of the people they are now oppressing; that caste and class barriers will be reduced to insignificance; that peasants will abruptly forsake the "wisdom" of their ancestors in favor of foreigners' technical advice; that corps of civil servants will suddenly spring out of nowhere, rejecting the corrupting influences of caste, clan, and graft, and dedicate themselves efficiently to the welfare of the community; that shrewd investors of capital will begin to risk their money in unpromising areas; that people will, in short, begin acting not just rationally, but even altruistically. Of course everyone hopes that these things will come to pass; but the Cornucopians have to assume that they will occur promptly—before the relentless sweep of unregulated population expansion makes all economic planning useless. They are expecting, in short, not just a miracle, but a whole set of miracles.

The Cornucopians are right to insist that production is an important part of the problem of underdevelopment. Population control by itself will fill no rice bowls. But, as Robert Heilbroner wrote in 1963, underdevelopment has complex causes; "It is not 'just' a lack of capital, or 'just' backward ways, or 'just' a population problem, or even 'just' a political problem, which weighs upon the poorer nations. It is a combination of all of these, each aggravating the other."[28]

Given this basic understanding, we should find it possible to recognize more than one approach to the problem. The dilemma of overpopulation-underdevelopment can be seen, from one point of view, as a matter of raising production to meet the demand, or, from another point of view, as a matter of limiting demand so that foreseeable production has a chance of satisfying it. In fact, we must see it both ways; to ignore either approach to the problem is to increase the already formidable chance of failure.

Chapter 3

Ideology (I): Communists and Overpopulation

> *Maybe it makes some sense to reduce
> the rate of increase of population in
> any economically backward country in
> order to increase to some extent the
> level of well-being . . . ? [We] give a
> sharp negative answer.*

—T. V. RYABUSHKIN[1]

Leningrad, 1963: Leonid, a young Soviet graduate student in architecture, is pointing to a florid Stalin-Gothic office building.

LEONID: That's "personality-cult" architecture; it's non-functional and over-decorated. Since Stalin's death we are free to build better.

I: Then you think that Premier Khrushchev's recent criticisms of the arts will not hamper your architects?

LEONID: Comrade Khrushchev's criticisms are only reminders of the duty of the artist to maintain contact with the people. He distills the opinions of the people and expresses them; since the Party and the people are one, he speaks *for* the people.*

I: Shouldn't artists be free to work out their creative ideas, even if the Party thinks they are wrong?

LEONID: Our artists *are* free. But they have to make sense.

I: Doesn't that mean their freedom is limited?

LEONID: No, their freedom is not limited—but they have to make sense. Khrushchev's warning was directed at the abstractionists, whose paintings have no social significance.

---

* The obvious irony of this remark, after the events of October, 1964, illustrates some of the difficulties involved in following an authoritarian ideology.

I: What is your opinion of Picasso's "Guernica"?

LEONID: The "Guernica" is a great painting. It has social significance, even though it has abstract elements.

The reader should be cautioned against trying to make strict sense of this conversation; it will yield little to such attempts. It represents, however, the flavor of several of my talks with Marxists, from Moscow to Tokyo. Genuine discussion rarely developed from these encounters, for it is not possible really to discuss a subject with people whose ideas are predetermined and doctrinaire. These talks had a certain interest, nevertheless, because they showed so graphically how minds tend to work when in the grip of an authoritarian ideology.

Of course, every nation has its ideology. Our own Constitution is thoroughly infused with what are properly called ideological propositions; all our talk about freedom, justice, and equality is ideological. But when a prevailing ideology is invested in an authoritarian power structure—whether political or religious—it changes from a mere rationale to a commandment, to which one must pay an unquestioning allegiance. When this happens, Authority takes on the vestments of Infallibility: doubts are subdued, inconsistencies are ignored or glossed over, and serious criticism becomes heresy or treason.

It is only by understanding the nature of authoritarian ideology that one can understand the Communists' opposition to population control, even in the face of a population explosion. Communists have simply never believed in overpopulation. Karl Marx called Malthus' theory a "libel on the human race" and "the great destroyer of all hankerings after human development"[2]— and Marx, of course, set the tone for subsequent Communist pronouncements. Chou-En-lai has referred with open contempt to "so-called population pressures,"[3] and Khrushchev labelled Malthusianism a "cannibalistic theory."[4] Recently E. K. Federov, Secretary General of the U.S.S.R. Academy of Sciences, argued that famines are not related to overpopulation but are only "one of the inheritances of colonialism. . . . The example of the Soviet Union and a series of other countries—weakly developed in the past—demonstrates in practice how economic development can far outstrip in its tempo the growth of population."[5] Soviet delegate T. V. Ryabushkin once told a United Nations conference, "The Malthusian theory is harmful because it distracts attention from really scientific ways of increase of the working people's well-being."[6]

Communism (so the theory goes) is such an effective economic system that it can provide for any given population. J. D. Bernal, an English scientist sympathetic to the Communist point of view, dismisses overpopulation in this way:

What has been done under the impetus of socialist ideas and practice already points to an enormous extension of civilization—agriculture and industry together—in which the soil will not merely be preserved but indefinitely improved, and the life it supports will be multiplied. In the light of this knowledge and experience, all the talk of the danger of over-population appears all the more clearly as reactionary non-sense.[7]

Starting with such propositions, the Communist propaganda apparatus has been directing a Utopian message to the underdeveloped countries. See what communism could do for you, it says: it could triple your farmland; could increase your yields; could make food out of grass; and so on. The theme of "could" is varied indefinitely, punctuated by strong notes of disapproval of the "reactionaries" who worry about population increase. For instance (to paraphrase the party line further): "The bourgeois economists only talk about 'overpopulation' to distract your attention from the real evil, which is colonialism"; or "The racist societies are only interested in limiting your numbers because they are afraid of being overrun by the dark-skinned people"; or "The capitalist societies are willing to violate the sanctity of human life for the protection of their private property."

The Big Battalions

> It must be considered reprehensible to withhold healthy children from the nation.
> —ADOLF HITLER, 1926

> What is the root cause of all our economic difficulties? It is the overpopulation of our territory.
> —ADOLF HITLER, 1939[8]

It has not been a habit of Westerners to take Communist pronouncements simply at face value; consequently, there has been a certain amount of voiced and unvoiced suspicion of the motives behind Communist encouragement of population expansion. The Russians are well past the 230 million mark; the Chinese have shot past 730 million. Both nations are still growing rapidly. In view of recent experience, totalitarian countries with high-birth policies cannot help but raise suspicions. Many of us remember all too vividly the high-birth policies of Hitler, Mussolini, and the Japanese—and the eventual call for *Lebensraum*. This comparison may be unfair, at least as far as the U.S.S.R. is concerned; one must hope so. But in a highly competitive world, it is only sensible to consider all the possibilities.

Regarding China, at this point in history, I do not think the suspicion is unfair. (Why, for instance, did Red China occupy Tibet?) Certainly a measure of Chinese chest-thumping derives from those 700-plus Chinese millions, who, according to Red Chinese propaganda, are not only a productive economic asset, not only a massive, potentially profitable group of consumers for the temptation of international trade, but even a force against which the hydrogen bomb itself is useless. One Chinese leader is supposed to have asserted that China need not fear World War III, since she would probably emerge from it with some 300 million survivors and would therefore soon dominate the world.

We are obliged to worry that the Communists are pursuing a policy of "big battalions," not only because we remember the tragic 1930's, but in view of militaristic policies throughout the world and throughout history. Communist generals are not alone, after all, in relishing large populations. A distinguished Egyptian demographer told me in 1963 that the military leaders there were against population limitation because "Egypt must become great"; an Indian demographer told me that since the Chinese invasion, Indian militarists have increasingly criticized the government's family planning program; a leader of the Family Planning Association in Thailand told me the army had been a powerful and effective foe of the organization there from the beginning; and an important Chinese government official on Formosa, which has one of the highest growth rates in the world, told me: "Our population increase means we *must* go back to the mainland. That's what we're working for."

The military mentality varies little from place to place. But are the generals right? Will large populations make for powerful nations? Certainly not in underdeveloped societies (Communist or non-Communist), for in an age of industrialization and technological change, neither a country's economy nor its military establishment profits from numbers alone. Cortez, with six hundred soldiers, could terrify and subdue myriads of Montezuma's Aztecs because he was supported by a superior technology. If there is a World War III, it will not be a matter of pitting man against man; it will be contested chiefly on the combatant Powers' economic and technological ability to afford, and to construct, vastly complex and vastly expensive instruments of mass destruction. Even the United States, the wealthiest and most technologically advanced nation on earth, is finding it difficult to afford and difficult to develop the kind of weapons it had projected; and the Soviet Union, too, according to some reports, has had to abandon parts of its elaborate and expensive space program.

The simplistic notion of "more people, more power" is a delusion; but a delusion people believe in can cause a lot of damage, and we should be prepared for that eventuality. What we should not do, of course, is to panic at the thought of the growing Communist populations. The simplest response to such

panic—that we must compete with them for numerical suprem-
acy—is economically and militarily unsound. If we want to
compete with the Communists, there are much better ways of
doing it than engaging in a dangerous and inauspicious breeding
contest.

The Uses of Proliferation

> America
>   wonders,
>   watches unblinking,
> America
>   measures
>   the U.S.S.R.
> What are
>   these Russians?
>   Of what rare breed?
> Beavering,
>   building,
>   making and tilling . . .
>   —VLADIMIR MAYAKOVSKY[9]

In 1851 Czar Nicholas I completed a most unusual railroad.
It runs between Moscow and Leningrad, and it runs the whole
distance—400 miles—in a straight line, because Nicholas insisted, despite engineers' logic, that he *wanted* it to run that way.
Today the crack Red Arrow Express speeds passengers over
the vast stretches of sparsely settled forest and plain that separate
the two cities, and as you make the trip you feel prompted to
ask, once more: where are the *people*?

The Soviet Union, with 230 million inhabitants, occupies one-
sixth of the earth's land area; its population averages out to about
twenty-seven people per square mile. If we compare this to fifty-
three in the United States or 550 in the United Kingdom, the
Soviet Union seems underpopulated—which reminds us that the
other great Communist Power, China, with about 200 people

per square mile, is much less densely populated than India, with 370, or Japan, with 660. There is some reason to believe, then, that the two leading Communist nations, who avowedly want to develop their vast territories further, may really be able to use more manpower than they now have.

To do so, however, both countries will have to overcome some formidable obstacles. That enormous sweep of little-used land between Moscow and Leningrad is not as promising as a casual summer tourist might suppose. It is low-lying land, and largely marshy. ("There is a greater proportion of marsh in Russia," wrote Bernard Pares in his classic history, "than anywhere else in Europe."[10]) Furthermore, it is in a northerly latitude. Moscow is north of the 55th parallel, which runs through southern Alaska. Leningrad is edged by the 60th parallel, which splits Oslo, Norway, skirts the northern tip of Scotland, and bisects the Hudson Bay. This is cold country—and vast stretches of the Soviet Union lie still north of the 60th parallel. Such land may serve for mining or forestry or even for some types of industry, but it can have only limited use as farmland.

China and the Soviet Union do, however, have little-used lands that are more promising. They both want to develop these lands thoroughly. For this they need capital. In *Das Kapital*, Marx put forth a doctrine of surplus value which proposes that the average worker's labor produces more than enough for his subsistence. This "more," this surplus, Marx said, has typically been kept by the exploiting capitalist employer. However, Marx did not propose that the worker deserved to keep all his earnings for himself. The right to surplus value belongs only to society-as-a-whole.

Therefore, according to this theory, the more people, the more surplus; and the more surplus, the more capital available for national development. The conclusion seems sound enough; but the premises are debatable. For every productive pair of hands there is also a hungry mouth, as well as a whole range of social necessities to be provided. Under what conditions can a developing country be sure that the hands will produce more than the mouth needs? In a totalitarian scheme of things, the answer is clear: society must *see to it* that the mouth consumes less than the hands produce—even if the hands are not producing very much. This is precisely the formula that both China and the U.S.S.R. have been following—although the Soviet people's demand for higher living standards finally forced Premier Khrushchev to compromise the formula to the extent of buying grain abroad. In doing so, however, he himself affirmed the existence of the formula. How was it possible to sell grain abroad in the Stalin era, he asked a plenary session of the Communist Party's Central Committee in 1963: "If grain were to be distributed . . . according to the method used by Stalin and Molotov, then we could have sold grain abroad this year, too. They sold grain while in some areas people had bloated stomachs or even died from lack of food."[11]

The formula, then, is not a gentle one. But the cold fact is that any developing country, communistic or not, needs to follow some such formula. Agriculture must (for the first time in most underdeveloped countries) produce a surplus, and do it with an ever smaller proportion of workers, so that labor can be diverted to industry. That is their only real hope for economic development.

The great problem in most non-communistic underdeveloped countries is to develop the social discipline necessary to make desperately poor people willing to do with even less than they now have, for the sake of a conceivably better life many years hence. It may well be that the industrialization of India and other such nations will founder on this very issue: how can a relatively free society develop and enforce such a stringent discipline?

China and the U.S.S.R. have the same problem, but their solution is comparatively clear-cut. A group of well-organized and dynamic leaders, invested with what amounts to total power, work out a master plan for the mobilization of human and physical resources: land is appropriated; factories are built; workers are mandatorily assigned to certain tasks; food is rationed; opposition is put down; and economic inertia (presumably) is thus overcome. Edgar Snow, the author of *Red Star over China* and *The Other Side of the River,* spent five months in mainland China in 1960. I spoke to him soon afterward. The Chinese, he said, were using their masses of people to create capital by working them to the breaking point of their physical endurance. ("Agony capital," economists have aptly called this.) René Dumont, a professor of agronomy with whom I talked at the University of Paris, had also recently been to China. He estimated that the peasants were being forced to work, in the course of a year, more than twice as long as they had worked in pre-Communist times. An ordinary British tourist in China reported in 1963:

A cart that is drawn by a bullock in India is pulled in China by men straining on ropes.

Aside from any humane considerations, the waste of manpower is immense. I saw nine men dragging a road-roller at snail's pace up a slope in Hankow; elsewhere, six men with three hand-carts were coping with a load suitable for one competent horse or ox.[12]

The mistake in this statement is the word "waste." If the Communist planners are more concerned about a future economic goal than about the pleasures and pains of their current population, then such work is not waste at all, but an efficient (however cold-blooded) use of the most readily available resource. Both China and the U.S.S.R. have had some success with this kind of planning. Some economists believe that China's current annual investment ratio may be as high as 30 per cent—a remarkable figure.[13]

Nevertheless, the Communists have not yet by any means found a formula for assured success in developing their under-developed areas. In post-Stalinist Russia there is apparently little enforced migration to Siberia, for instance, and not enough people are going there willingly. When you have seen a dozen typical Russian villages—little collections of dingy, unpainted log houses intersected by dirt streets, cluttered with wood piles, and with a dirt road leading off into an otherwise trackless plain toward some distant civilization—you can understand why the Siberian hinterlands do not inspire enthusiasm. Pioneering is not a popular twentieth-century sport. Highly trained people are no more likely in the Soviet Union than in India or Egypt to want to spend their lives in backward areas. Those Russians who do go to Siberia are frequently unhappy, and six out of ten come back.[14]

Moscow, on the other hand, is comparatively attractive, and so many people have crowded into that city that it is in the throes of a monumental housing problem. The Soviets see no end to this problem in the near future, and as a defense against further immigration, have made Moscow a closed city; it is all but impossible for a Soviet citizen to get permission to move there.

Developing the virgin areas of the Soviet Union, especially areas where nature is hostile, is quite costly. The Soviets are more cautious now than they used to be about sending people to the less inviting parts of Siberia, where they have to create and supply whole new communities at great expense. Also, in a specialized society, manpower alone is not enough. Sheer muscle can of course pull a cart or a road roller, but that is a far cry from modern agriculture or industry. Too many of the Communist millions are functionally illiterate—they simply don't know enough to be efficient farmers or workers. That is why an American agricultural specialist I talked with in Moscow was skeptical of the Soviet leaders' professed desire to have yet another hundred million workers. It isn't more hands they need at this point, he said; it's more brains, more skill at all levels. This applies not only to tractor-driving and combine-operating but also to the upper echelons of officialdom, where there is a great deal of ambitious talk but too little effectiveness at converting ideas into actions—at actually getting things done.

Thus, while it may be that the Russians and Chinese have surveyed their populations and their potentialities and have concluded that Marxist theories about population and surplus value will work for them, this is not the only possible conclusion. Marxists frequently point to what they consider inner contradictions in capitalistic societies. On the subject of overpopulation, however, the contradictions (using the word in a slightly different sense) of the Communists' position are so important and so much glossed over that they require close inspection.

Contradiction No. 1: The Philosophy-of-Could versus Communist Failures

> Officially, contradictions do not exist in the minds of the citizens in the people's democracies. Nobody dares to reveal them publicly. And yet the question of how to deal with them is posed in real life.
>
> —CZESLAW MILOSZ[15]

To quote Secretary General Federov again," The possibilities mankind has to influence nature increase at a faster rate than man's numerical increase."[16] "Possibilities": with this word we are once more in the wonderland of the Cornucopian economists. Both in China and the U.S.S.R., strenuous efforts have been made to increase agricultural output in order to feed burgeoning populations. Leaders of both nations have pointed with pride to the expansion of cultivated areas and improvement of agricultural methods as evidence that population growth need not concern them seriously. But in fact neither country has been consistently effective as a food producer. In the U.S.S.R., local shortages of food have been a chronic complaint, and, over the last half-century, food production has actually lagged behind population growth.[17] (Distribution is better than in czarist times and starvation is apparently a thing of the past—but that is, for the moment, irrelevant; we are concerned now with production.) Since 1960, Soviet economists and politicians have openly complained of deficiencies in their agricultural program.

Walking the neighborhoods of Moscow and Leningrad in 1963, I soon saw why. Winding through the interiors of shops and snaking out in block-long lines onto the windy sidewalks, there were dozens, scores, and even (it seems incredible now) hundreds of Russians, waiting to buy simple necessities. Inside the food stores, what does the Soviet consumer have to choose

from? In the barnlike central market of Moscow, I found only a
sparse selection of low-grade meats; vegetables so stunted and
scabby that they probably could not be sold at all in American
markets; no fruits (this was in April) except dried ones and a
few oranges and apples. The prices were memorable: the oranges
were selling for fifty cents apiece, the better apples for forty
cents; the little lettuce that was available was selling for $2.75
a pound, cucumbers for $2.25 a pound. (This is according to the
artificially high exchange rate for dollars, but since the average
Soviet worker earns only about $100 a month, the price would
seem at least as high to a Russian as to an American.) As a
result, the Russian diet is very low in meat, butter, and fresh
green vegetables, and very high in starchy foods. Since my return
in 1963, news agencies have reported that the sale of bread
(the most important single item in the Russian diet) has been
subject to new restrictions, retail sales of wheat flour have been
discontinued entirely, milk production has reverted to the 1958
level, and 41 per cent of all the pigs in the country were slaugh-
tered prematurely because they could not be fed.

Can Soviet agriculture do better? On a collective farm I
heard a spokesman predict that production would soon increase
because of more mechanization, greater use of chemical fertilizers,
and (astonishingly, I thought) "planting fewer non-productive
crops on inappropriate lands."* But an American agricultural
expert in Moscow was less sanguine. In fact, he told me, Soviet
agriculture is all but hopeless, partly because it is attempting
to blueprint, on a national scale, an occupation that is essentially
ad hoc. Factories can be planned with some accuracy at long
range; farms have to be managed at close range and with considerable flexibility. The chances of getting significantly more and
better meat, fruit, and vegetables in the foreseeable future are, he
said, very dim.

Against that background, it is hardly surprising that the
Soviet Union has recently had to buy millions of bushels of
wheat from Western countries. Humanitarians must hope that
Soviet agriculture will eventually produce better crops for the

---

* After Khrushchev's ouster, his successors listed, among his "hare-
brained schemes," the planting of corn where it would not grow.

Russian people. But there is no immediate prospect of it; the philosophy-of-could has not proved any more convincing in the mouths of Communists than in the mouths of conservative Western Cornucopians.

But if the U.S.S.R. is in serious agricultural trouble, China is in a worse situation. Like all American passports, mine was stamped "not valid for travel to or in Communist . . . China"; so I had to be content with the synthetic China of Hong Kong and Formosa. At least one part of this experience was authentic, however: the food. Chinese cuisine is often called the best in the world: tasty and varied, rich in soups, ingenious with duck and pork, fragrant with herbs and seasonings. A dinner at which I was a guest demonstrated Chinese resourcefulness: shark fin soup, bamboo shoot soup, mushroom and chicken soup, ham, abalone, smoked meat, duck, shrimp with walnuts, chicken livers, kidneys with broccoli, minced pigeon and peas on rice, barbecued chicken, deep-fried duck, steamed fish, noodles with shredded chicken, and hot pudding. All that at one sitting.

Ironically and tragically, the nation that had the ingenuity to invent such a meal has never solved a more basic problem: how to keep all of its people adequately fed all of the time. The Chinese have made great claims and have issued impressive agricultural statistics—but meanwhile their food supplies have failed to keep pace with their growing number of mouths, and, even before the Soviets, they had to resort to buying Western grain. Through the middle 1950's, reports of bad crop years persisted. In 1958, however, there was a good crop, and the Chinese instituted the agricultural commune as a part of their "great leap forward."

But the commune, a vast, highly organized, super-collective community, did not leap. Harvests were bad again the next year —and the next—and the next. Finally in 1962 Premier Chou announced plans to persuade the newer urban workers to return to agricultural work; the commune system was revised into more manageable "production teams"; and crop yields have now apparently improved somewhat. But over the last ten years—most of them "bad"—China's population has increased by about 130 million, which makes any so-called crop "victory" now a highly qualified thing.

I hope it is clear that I am not concerned here with merely placing blame. It is irrelevant to my argument whether the Communists' agricultural failures have been due mostly to bad weather (as the Communists say) or to bad management (as some Westerners think). What I do want to emphasize is that rapidly growing nations are not going to be fed upon ideologically-inspired promises. When human beings look to the future with the hopeful words, "Look what we 'could' do," the assumption is always that we *will* do it. We tend, illogically but incurably, to be optimists. But possibilities are not performances; the only way the Communists can vindicate their philosophy-of-could is by transforming their claims into realities—and that they have not yet been able to do.

The Communists are right in wanting to harness science to production more effectively than in the past. They are right in saying that distribution should be more equitable than it has been. But they have yet to prove that their system can keep production ahead of runaway population growth.

Contradiction No. 2: Party Line and Party Practice

> Tsze-kung asked what constituted the superior man. The Master said, "He acts before he speaks, and afterward speaks according to his actions."
>
> —CONFUCIUS[18]

In 1957 the Chinese surprised the rest of the world by openly sponsoring a national program of birth control, "in order to lighten consumption by non-producers during the present period of socialist construction."[19] Then, for reasons that have never been made clear (though presumably the good harvest of 1958 and the "great leap forward" had a lot to do with it), the program was suddenly abandoned. The intriguing thing is that it was ever made public at all, for it revealed to the world that current Communist thinking on the subject of population control is not as straightforward as their party line would have it. In fact, this is a point upon which professed Communist doctrine and actual Communist practice are now persistently divergent. Edgar Snow has said that Premier Chou and the Chinese Minister of Health have both told him that large families are now generally frowned upon in the upper circles. In *The Other Side of the River*, Snow writes: "The two-child family is regarded as ideal and party functionaries receive no extra allowances for more children."[20] Furthermore, Snow told me, there is a vast contraceptive industry in China; contraceptives are plentiful and easily available; and they sell for one-tenth of U.S. prices.

As time passes, we get increasingly firm evidence that China, while overtly clinging to Marxist theory on overpopulation, is actually engaged in a national, government-sponsored birth control campaign. In May, 1963, a Shanghai newspaper mentioned a Planned Birth Work Committee, set up to organize "mass propaganda and education in planned birth" through factories, communes, schools, and street committees.[21] The government is now encouraging research in contraceptive methods and more efficient sales of the available ones. Late marriage, sterilization of husbands, and spacing of children are being publicly urged. In 1964 Chou told Edgar Snow frankly that he was studying Japanese population-control methods and hoped to reduce China's growth rate.[22]

Other Communist countries reveal similar patterns. It has never been very difficult to obtain an abortion in the U.S.S.R., and in 1955 it became legal to do so. Two years later, after a flood of requests, the Soviet Minister of Health called for vigorous scientific research into the development of new contraceptive methods. Today the small family has become the ideal in Soviet cities. Contraception is now widespread, and Soviet doctors are reportedly experimenting with a new, non-hormonal oral contraceptive.

Poland, that independent, well-nigh heretical Communist nation, has its own population problem, and, unlike more orthodox Communist countries, has set up an official, government-sponsored family planning association (nicely called the "Institute of Conscious Motherhood"). There is also a state manufacturer of contraceptives, including the oral type, and even public coin-operated dispensing machines for distributing them. The director of the Institute of Conscious Motherhood told me that Poland, like the U.S.S.R., recognizes the need for birth control, partly as an alternative to a very high rate of abortions.

There are similar activities throughout Communist Eastern Europe. In 1960, delegates from Communist Bulgaria, Czechoslovakia, East Germany, Hungary, Poland, and Yugoslavia met with delegates from non-Communist countries, ostensibly to discuss abortion, and concluded unanimously that contraception is the best way not only to prevent abortions but also to "balance population trends in relation to the economic needs of individual countries."

What are we to make of such contradictions? Do they mean that Communist doctrine on this subject has been gradually and naturally evolving—as, for instance, the doctrines of the Protestant churches have been? "The science of Marxism," a young Soviet economist told me in Moscow, is gradually changing; and perhaps "in concrete situations" it might change with respect to overpopulation. But there is this essential difference between the Protestants and the Marxists: the churches are preaching what they want practiced; whereas the Communists are now officially preaching one thing and actually practicing another. On the one hand, Communists scoff at fears of overpopulation in the densely populated, underdeveloped countries; on the other hand, the Communist governments of the U.S.S.R., China, and other countries are officially developing and making available methods of population control in their own less densely populated lands. The question is, why? And the answer may lie where so many answers to Communist puzzles seem to lie: deep in the maze of Communist nations' foreign policies. To examine this possibility, we must look at yet another contradiction.

Contradiction No. 3: Overt Benevolence and Covert Ruthlessness

> In the national struggles of the
> proletarians of the different coun-
> tries, [the Communists] bring to
> the front the common interests of
> the entire proletariat . . .
> —MARX and ENGELS[23]

The missionary message of Communism is chiefly directed to the "common man," whose lot, in most countries, varies only in degrees of wretchedness. To these people the Communists therefore project an image of benevolence and repeat their philosophy-of-could, the promise of a better life. Are these humanitarian declarations sincere? Or are they perhaps a calculated means to the ulterior end of Communist expansion? There is a simple test in this case. The Communists consistently maintain that only under communism can the common man expect a horn of plenty, that only communism can cope with rapidly expanding populations. On strictly humanitarian grounds, then, the Communists should support policies of population control in non-Communist countries and ignore population control in their own countries.

The fact is just the opposite. The Communists have been officially opposing population control in all societies, even in those underdeveloped nations which are more densely populated, faster growing, and less well supplied with land, resources, and industry than are the U.S.S.R. and China, and where overpopulation is substantially to blame for people's misery. At the U.N. World Population Conference in 1954, for instance, the Soviets officially condemned contraception, and at a subsequent conference of the U.N. Economic Commission for Asia and the Far East, the Soviet delegation was the only one to oppose the promotion of birth control in Asia.[24] As late as 1962, when the U.N. General Assembly debated the subject of population growth and economic development, the Soviet Union "expounded the traditional Communist position that Western discussions of the population problem were based on 'neo-Malthusian fallacies' and that population problems ceased to exist under Communism."[25]

All this seems to me to indicate that the Communists are acting on anti-humanitarian principles, that they are actually promoting working-class misery in non-communistic countries—presumably because if non-communistic systems perform badly, they may be replaced by communistic ones. The more men (relative to employment) that there are in a country's working force, after all, the lower wages will be driven; the more people there are (relative to national wealth), the lower per-capita incomes will be. President Ayub Khan of Pakistan recently said, "If we continue to increase at the present rate, it will ultimately lead to a standard of living which will be little better than that of animals."[26] Thus, to promote overpopulation in the underdeveloped nations is to promote misery there and consequently, "inevitably," communism. Mao Tse Tung has declared that poverty is a positive asset to the Communists because it generates "revolutionary fervor."[27] And Communists everywhere have therefore opposed American aid programs, which aim at solving problems quietly and reducing revolutionary fervor.

Although they claim to be against population control on principle, then, the Communists are nevertheless taking steps to check their own population growth, apparently in order to improve economic conditions; and although they preach "the sanctity of life" to underdeveloped countries, their official opposition to population control is actually making life in such countries more and more degraded and miserable. Thus an ostensible Marxist belief does double duty as a ruthless Cold War tactic.

The Appeal of Communism

> It was mainly on account of all the
> misery and hardship I'd been
> through that I became a Com-
> munist. To me communism meant
> work for everybody, salvation for
> everybody . . .
>
> —SICILIAN WORKER[28]

In the course of a talk with Prime Minister Nehru, an
American student once asked if "international communism will
threaten Asian democracy." Nehru replied firmly (in an uninten-
tional paraphrase of Mao), "Communism ultimately grows, not
from external pressures, but from very backward conditions in
the economy." Driven by constant hunger, often unable to find
work, stunted by illiteracy, hounded by debt, tormented by disease: the lot of the underprivileged people, the majority of mankind, has never been a happy one. Nevertheless, most of these
wretched people have usually been quiescent, partly because they
lacked the energy to rebel against their misery and partly because
the misery has been so permanent and so widespread as to seem
the natural order of things.

The great change that has been taking place since World
War II is that people everywhere are discovering that their
misery is not heaven-sent, not in the natural order of things, but
the result of ignorance, prejudice, mismanagement, or greed. The
knowledge has spread that it is now technically possible for
everyone to have enough to eat and to wear. People in Asia, in
Africa, and in Latin America have *found out*—and are becoming
considerably less quiet about their desperation; they want things
and are demanding them. That is what has created the revolution of rising expectations.

American aid to underdeveloped countries is intended to
enable them eventually to stand on their own feet, to grow
stronger economically and politically. But we have not always

seen this problem in its most relevant terms. To talk about "fighting communism," for instance, by exporting guns or surplus food is partially to miss the point. Guns, though sometimes necessary, are never enough, because meeting only the military threat of communism is treating only a symptom; the real disease is poverty and discontent. Our food surpluses are not enough, either, because, seen from the point of view of the world's need, they are only a small drop in a deep bucket. If we exported all of our surplus food, every year, to the malnourished peoples, it would only be the equivalent of about a teacupful of rice per person per week.[29]

Even our medical aid, through the World Health Organization and otherwise, which seems a perfectly straightforward attempt to ease the pressures of discontent on the people of the underdeveloped nations, has often had unexpected political consequences. In Thailand, for instance, we have helped in various ways to reduce disease and death; as a result, the population there has spurted spectacularly. There is not enough work for the increased population, which is now drifting from the villages to the cities to form great pools of unemployed and therefore disgruntled people. One up-country Thai mayor told an American, only half in jest, that he hoped malaria would *not* be eliminated there; he was afraid of what would happen, socially and politically, when so many unemployed men regained their health and energy.

Of course this is not meant to disparage humanitarian efforts to strike at disease. "After all," a smiling Nehru once said, "we can't permit bad health in order to reduce the population." Nehru himself recognized, nevertheless, that overpopulation is at the very base of many of the underdeveloped nations' other problems. The Communists can be depended upon to take political advantage of these problems.

Chapter 4

Ideology (II): Conservative Catholics and Birth Control

I have just given birth to my seventh child. She will give glory to God forever by the very fact of her existence.

—LETTER TO THE AUTHOR

FROM A ROMAN CATHOLIC MOTHER

In Hong Kong the population problem is so obvious that it looks like a classroom exhibit. Because of its high birth rate and its influx of refugees, the colony now holds twice as many people as it did twenty years ago. There are no longer enough houses for everyone, nor enough jobs, nor enough schools or teachers, nor enough water, nor enough food; thousands are kept from starvation by relief handouts from the United States and British governments and other groups. Like Calcutta, Hong Kong might well be a presage of the Asian "City of the Future." Could anyone in that harassed city fail to see the dangers of too many people?

I visited a Roman Catholic relief center there, where American government-supplied surplus food was being distributed by a priest to long lines of destitute Chinese. This same priest has written a novel to which he put this prologue:

I work among the Chinese refugees. I visit them in their huts on the hill slopes. Each hut is bursting with life. I have seen how new refugees have been cordially accommodated. There is always room for relatives or friends from the same village in China.

I have seen the new arrivals gather old boards or cast off pieces of wood from new buildings under construction. I have met them at the wharves picking up old wooden boxes, pieces of tar paper and sheets of tin thrown away by transportation companies. Later I watched them after working hours, busy as bees putting up their own huts on the hillsides.

I frequently see mothers sitting in the doorways of their huts doing piece work; putting wrist bands together, sewing buttons on shirts, sewing gloves together, and making artificial flowers.[1]

There is a strangely surrealistic quality about this scene— the accordion-like expansiveness of those "bursting" huts, the energetic people busy at building, and no doubt whistling while they work, the women patiently sewing—for every detail is a caricature of the squalor and degradation of the *real* scene: the ugly tarpaper shacks, the uncomfortable and unsanitary over-crowding, the tedious, fiercely competitive, low-paid piece work. The priest's happy tableau is like one of those cheerfully fraudu-lent travelogues of "picturesque natives," which transmute misery into radiant technicolor. All is well, he seems to imply, as long as the shacks are "bursting with life"—after all, "there is always room" for more.

But what is it really like to be a mother, sitting in the door of a ramshackle hut, making artificial flowers? An American nun in the Catholic relief center had worked directly with these flower-makers since the business began. "At first it worked very well," she told me, "because we were in the artificial flower business early. But then more and more people took it up and prices went down. Now the competition is terrible and it's almost impossible to get a price that will provide a decent living. That is the evil of competition here in Hong Kong."

Another nun, a nurse in a Roman Catholic school in Hong Kong, told me that the biggest health problem among their children is with diseases related to malnutrition. The children often come to school without food, she said, and are under-standably apathetic about their class work. A particularly serious disease among the refugees is tuberculosis, which is almost impossible to control because the "squatters" are so crowded together in those little shacks—where "there is always room . . ."

Later, at lunch with the priest, I asked him: didn't he think rapid population growth in Asia was cause for concern? "Growth is essential," he replied. But wasn't this population growth giving rise to serious economic and moral problems? "The human brain will solve any problems," he said. Didn't these problems seem actually to be getting worse rather than better? "Don't be afraid of them," he insisted; "the more problems there are, the more inventive people will be."

Msgr. John C. Knott, Director of the Family Life Bureau of the National Catholic Welfare Conference, wrote in 1963, "The mind of the Church has been and is in favor of life. She is not frightened by the statistical data presented by demographers and described in nightmare terms by propagandists."[2] His unconscious paraphrase of the priest in Hong Kong was no coincidence; both comments are examples of ideological thinking, and are, I believe, particularly harmful ones. The Roman Catholic Church, still dominated by its conservative traditions and conservative theologians, is the only Western institution of any importance that is consciously and actively obstructing population limitation. This is not only a great social misfortune for the underdeveloped countries; I believe that if the Church does not modify its position soon, it will also be a great moral misfortune for the Church, and that Roman Catholics of the future will look back on our times with shame and disbelief.

How Natural Is "Natural Law"?

> Numberless are the world's wonders, but none
> More wonderful than man; the stormgray sea
> Yields to his prows, the huge crests bear him high;
> Earth, holy and inexhaustible, is graven
> With shining furrows where his plows have gone . . .
> —SOPHOCLES[3]

The Roman Catholic Church, while permitting the regulation of births by a complicated and highly unreliable system called the "rhythm method," has traditionally opposed what it terms "artificial" birth control as (in the words of Pope Pius XI) "an offense against the law of God and of nature."[4] This law of nature, or natural law, is, according to the *Catholic Encyclopedia*, "the rule of conduct which is prescribed to us by the Creator in the constitution of the nature with which He has endowed us." Presumably this law "binds everyone, Catholic and non-Catholic alike"; presumably it can be discovered by reason alone; but also presumably it can be infallibly interpreted only by the Roman Catholic Church.

The key to the Catholic position on natural law is that human reason, unaided by divine revelation, should be able to ascertain what that law is. It can be put this way: God endowed man with reasoning powers capable of understanding His works; God indicates His intentions in those works; therefore man can discover God's intentions. This is an appealing idea, and not only to theologians. Plato and Aristotle were attracted to it. The poet Wordsworth proposed that "To her fair works did Nature link/ The human soul" and that even the memory of a landscape could cause man to "see into the life of things." The astronomer Kepler assumed that, as his biographer put it, "the mind repeated the thoughts which God had materialized in His Creation," Kepler himself saying, "we astronomers are priests of the highest God in regard to the book of nature . . ."[5] And Jefferson and his colleagues thought it "self-evident" that rights had been granted to men by the "Laws of Nature and of Nature's God."

The necessary assumption behind natural law, then, is that nature's moral lessons are clear enough for reasonable people to understand; people should, therefore, agree on them. If this assumption were correct, the case for natural law would be strong indeed. However, the assumption is not correct—not for poets, nor for scientists, nor for politicians, nor for theologians. The language of the *Catholic Encyclopedia* sounds precise and even legalistic ("the rule of conduct which is prescribed to us by the Creator in the constitution of the nature . . ." and so on). Catholic spokesmen usually sound juristic when they define natural law: "The natural law," writes one theologian, "is the statement of the inner principles of action, placed in man by God in making man what he is, and demanded by the very nature of man so that his human activity may direct him to that perfection which is proper to his human nature."[6] But unless there is a widespread agreement, a genuine consensus, on this "rule of conduct,"

on these "inner principles of action," the legalisms are reduced to
dressed-up and institutionalized ways of putting such simple and
personal opinions as "This is natural" and "That's not natural."
Without a consensus, they cannot pretend to be more than that.

Of course there is no such consensus, which is why, in the
end, Catholic theologians are forced (in practice, not in principle) to abandon the idea that natural law can be perceived by
reason, unaided by divine revelation; and at this point they fall
back on authority. Acute theologians can sophisticate and therefore disguise this retreat, as when John Courtney Murray, S.J.,
writes that consensus "is not 'majority opinion' . . . it looks for its
validity, not to the sheer fact that . . . people at large agree on it,
but to the evidence adduced to show that it is true . . ."[7] But
since it is the Church which judges the evidence, this turns out,
in the long run, to be simply an involved way of putting the case
for authority—for asserting, as Pope Pius XI wrote, that "God . . .
has appointed the Church to be the guardian and teacher of all
truth concerning faith and morals."[8] It is this kind of thinking
that apparently caused Michael Novak, a brilliant Catholic
writer, to complain recently, in a Jesuit publication: "Many of us
find it almost impossible to argue with priests, too many of whom
retreat too soon to authority."[9]

On the question of authority, of course, opinion is divided.
Few non-Catholics agree with the Roman Catholic Church's con-
ception of natural law. Some of the things that seem natural to
many people, they hold, are contrary to Christian teaching;
indeed, a substantial part of the world's religious thought,
whether Hindu, Buddhist, Moslem, or Christian (including Roman Catholic), is aimed at curbing certain parts of what seems
our "inner nature." Neither can we take lessons from external
nature, for there we could find justification for almost anything
we pleased. In fact, says Karl Barth, an eminent Protestant
theologian, all analogies between God and this world are
meaningless; therefore it is impossible to discover what God
intended for us by examining either nature or ourselves.[10] It is
not appropriate, Protestants argue, to use sense perceptions about
a finite world to investigate the intentions of a cosmic God. God,
being infinite, can be known only by revelation.

Thus on the specific issue of birth control there is bound to be broad philosophical disagreement. The National Council of Churches of Christ in America, representing twenty-five major Protestant bodies, issued this statement in 1961: "Most of the Protestant churches hold contraception and periodic continence to be morally right when the motives are right. . . . motives, rather than methods, form the primary moral issue . . ."[11] Also, many individual Protestant denominations (Episcopal, Baptist, Disciples, Lutheran, Methodist, Presbyterian, Friends, Unitarian Universalist, and others) and Jewish groups have officially endorsed "artificial" birth control.

One Protestant theologian, Emil Brunner, holds that to define the purpose of sexual intercourse in terms of procreation is a semi-ascetic point of view without support in the New Testament.[12] Episcopal Bishop James A. Pike agrees. "Many Protestant theologians," he writes,

are no longer able to accept the premise that procreation is the only primary function of the sex act. One sometimes hears the statement that there are at least two "primary functions"—which, of course, is only an ungrammatical way of saying that there is no *primary* function. According to this view, the sex act is a sacramental means of expressing love between a man and a woman, in which "the twain become one flesh." Under certain circumstances this act may result in procreation, but even if it does not, the sacramental nature of marriage has been expressed therein.[13]

"All human history," writes the Protestant Reinhold Niebuhr,

is, in fact, a bewildering compound of natural impulse and necessity and human invention and intervention. These facts are so obvious in a technical age that one hopes that the [Roman Catholic] Church will ultimately bow to the inevitable. The [birth control] issue is at present a source of tension between the Church and modern society.[14]

"Human invention and intervention" to save lives is now taken for granted. There was a time when this was not so—when some kinds of death control were more controversial than birth control. During the Middle Ages more than one official Council of the Catholic Church forbade surgery to priests and monks. Likewise, Catholic theologians at the University of Paris once solemnly condemned inoculation.[15] The history of the Roman

Catholic Church is full of uncertainties about what is or is not natural: for instance, medieval Catholics thought that taking interest on money was "against nature," because money was "barren" and could not "breed" money.

But customs change and what seems natural or unnatural to one generation may seem the opposite to the next. A natural law is only natural and a law to those who happen to agree upon it. To others it may reasonably seem neither natural nor binding. Paul Quay, a Jesuit theologian, admits that "Few arguments in the domain of morality seem as unpersuasive to the great majority of Americans as the customary natural-law arguments against contraception . . ."[16] This is partly because we are, and have always been, constantly engaged in a running battle with nature on both the moral and the physical level. To say that offspring are the natural end of marriage, then, is true, but it is only true in the sense that bread and beef (or headaches and hangovers) are natural; they are all brought into being by the day-to-day activities of men and women. They can all therefore be increased or decreased by human forethought, according to the biddings of our intelligence and our conscience.

Of course it is precisely man's conscience and intelligence that have created this whole argument. Father Quay has attacked birth control as being a part of "the *lie* that man is his own master, that man bears dominion over himself, that man may subject his person and his nature to ends (or idols) of his own fashioning rather than those ordained by God's creative act."[17] While in New Delhi I mentioned this argument to Colonel B. L. Raina, the army surgeon in charge of the national family planning program. "Catholics tell me we are disobeying God," he said, "but I answer that God's greatest gift is intelligence. We are constantly improving our life by our own inventiveness."

Man is indeed forever mastering his environment by altering the conditions of his life out of nature's course: we manufacture clothing to keep ourselves warm, build levees to restrain rivers, drain swamps to improve agriculture and health, synthesize drugs to kill bacteria, fell trees to build houses where we may take refuge from nature, and so on. Such arguments, Roman Catholic theologians reply, are irrelevant because there is no purpose perceived by reason in permitting swamps to exist or rivers to run unchecked. Whereas, they insist, it is reasonable to conclude that the primary function of sex is for procreation.

This sounds suspiciously circular (reasonableness is sought in nature; nature must conform to reason), but overlooking that complication for the moment, let us ask: who is the best judge as to whether an act is natural and therefore (presumably) reasonable? Clearly it is whoever best understands nature. The question then becomes: who best understands nature? Is it the Church? For an informed answer, we must look to history.

Nature is all around us. It can be inspected by anyone, and presumably the Church, with its emphasis on natural law, wants it inspected keenly and responsibly. ("Natural law," writes an eminent sociologist, "presumes inquiry."[18]) That does not mean, however, that the Church has been consistently accurate in its study of nature. The early Church held, for instance, that the earth was the center of the universe and that the stars were brought out by God from his treasure house each evening and hung in the sky; St. Philastrius declared any other view heretical and "false to the Catholic faith." Peter Lombard, a noted Catholic professor and Archbishop of Paris, once declared in an influential manual that: "Just as man is made for the sake of God— that is, that he may serve Him—so the universe is made for the sake of man—that is, that it may serve *him*; therefore is man placed at the middle point of the universe, that he may both serve and be served."[19] This somewhat less than accurate reading of nature prevailed for centuries. When finally Galileo began teaching Copernicus' theory of heliocentricity, Copernicus' greatest book was condemned and placed on the Catholic *Index* of prohibited books, and Galileo was forbidden to discuss it. Eventually the Church summoned him before the Inquisition, where theologians declared his proposition that the earth revolves about the sun "absurd, false in philosophy, and, from a theological point of view at least, opposed to the true faith."[20] Instead, the Church approved arguments such as this: "Animals, which move, have limbs and muscles; the earth has no limbs or muscles, therefore it does not move. It is angels who make Saturn, Jupiter, the sun, etc., turn round . . ." Another argument began: "The Copernican theory of the earth's motion *is against the nature of the earth itself* . . ."[21]

The moral should be clear: "If natural law is to be usable," writes Brand Blanshard, "we must be able to tell what is natural."[22] But the Roman Catholic Church has demonstrated again and again that its knowledge of nature is not necessarily accurate. Any conclusions it reaches about natural law, therefore, are based upon fallible premises and must themselves be fallible and debatable.

Even if the Church had a reasonably good understanding of nature, though, it still would not follow that Church authorities would necessarily deduce an unmistakable "law" from it, for the simple reason that nature is an ambiguous guide. John Stuart Mill developed an extensive critique of the argument that nature offers God-given moral guidance:

Nature impales men, breaks them as if on the wheel, casts them to be devoured by wild beasts, burns them to death, crushes them with stones . . . starves them with hunger, freezes them with cold . . . with the most supercilious disregard both of mercy and of justice . . . A single hurricane destroys the hopes of a season; a flight of locusts, or an inundation, desolates a district . . . Everything, in short, which the worst men commit either against life or property is perpetrated on a larger scale by natural agents.[23]

Thus the Church must choose those parts of nature that it will accept as a guide. And of course it always chooses the parts it sees fit to choose, some aspects of nature being (apparently) more natural than others. Such choosing is necessarily arbitrary. As Mill said, "Either it is right that we should kill because nature kills; torture because nature tortures; ruin and devastate because nature does the like; or we ought not to consider at all what nature does, but what it is *good* to do."[24]

To argue the point at such length may seem like belaboring the obvious, but this is no butterfly on my wheel. The above arguments seem to me sensible enough, but I am aware that an energetic Catholic theologian could, if he wished, quickly raise enough counter-arguments to reassure himself that the traditional Catholic position was tenable and that birth control should there-fore still be opposed. I hope, though, that at least some of these potential opponents will pause in their work long enough to ask themselves a grave question: *ought* they to sit comfortably in their studies, offering themselves verbal assurances that all is well—or ought they perhaps to put down their pens, throw open their study doors, and listen with open hearts to the wail of a miserable world—in pain partly on their account?

People in all parts of the world are becoming increasingly aware that uncontrolled, "natural" human sex can seriously threaten man's efforts to improve his life. Rain is a blessing; floods are disasters. Control of births, it is more and more obvious, is the only realistic defense against the rising floods of population growth. I contend that human beings should not have to go on suffering for the sake of "natural law."

Catholic Conservatism and the Spread of Immorality

> They who see sin where there is no sin, and see no sin where there is sin, such men . . . enter the evil path.
>
> —THE BUDDHA[25]

Catholic opposition to birth control is not based solely on arguments relating to natural law. The Reverend Arthur Mc-Cormack, discussing an oral contraceptive in a Catholic Truth Society pamphlet, declares, "This pill will be social and moral dynamite. There is no guarantee that it will be used in the way that the population planners wish. In fact, there is every likelihood that, like present contraceptives, it will be used largely by those for whom it is NOT intended, with deplorable effects on morals."[26]

This is a common argument, and deserves examination. First of all, it should be pointed out that any objection to the immorality of contraceptives must apply equally to the Catholic-approved rhythm system. In fact, as Alvah Sulloway has suggested, the chance of promiscuity is considerably greater with the rhythm method than with contraceptives, since it is easily available to anyone, married or unmarried.[27]

It is also philosophically important to point out that although Father McCormack mentions morality, he is not really talking about moral issues. A moral choice is a decision between certain alternatives on the basis of their rightness or wrongness; it is not a compulsion to act in a certain way because of the fear of consequences. " 'What is done' and 'what is not done,' " writes the Rev. Dr. William Lillie, an authority on ethics, "may not be moral matters at all. . . . A man who does good deeds simply . . . from outside pressure can hardly be regarded as truly virtuous."[28] A woman who refrains from illicit sexual intercourse only because of fear of detection is not a moral woman, merely a cautious one. Such a misuse of contraceptives as Father McCormack fears would therefore have no moral significance. It might reveal immorality, but it could not cause it.

Conversely, it should also be noted that the absence of contraceptives does not guarantee either morality or prudence. Msgr. George A. Kelly, Director of the Family Life Bureau of the Roman Catholic Archdiocese of New York, declared in 1963 that because of birth control pills, 75 per cent of all young girls "won't be virgins" in 1980.[29] His assumption is, obviously, that contraceptives cause promiscuity. Whatever truth there may be in this assumption, it cannot be the whole story. Latin America, for instance, is predominantly Roman Catholic, and Catholic influence has made contraceptives difficult to obtain in many places there. At the same time, the highest rates of illegitimate births in the world are in Latin America, where consensual, or common-law, unions are frequent. In eight Latin American nations, more than half of all births are illegitimate. Furthermore, a recent survey in Santiago, Chile, revealed that more than one-fourth of all Chilean women admitted to having had induced abortions. The lack of contraceptives does not seem to create elevated standards of sexual behavior.

Indeed, for sincere Roman Catholics everywhere, the Church's position on birth control is itself having morally corrosive effects. The Church's arguments are simply not convincing to many of its own members, who, faced with a choice between the unreliable rhythm method and really effective contraceptives, are deciding more and more frequently to use contraceptives, from fear of having more children than they can properly care for. Some of my Catholic friends around the country have told me how corrupting this dilemma has been: to be consciously aware that they are sinning (and, in some cases, keeping this continuing sin hidden from their confessors) works to undermine their entire ethical footing. Psychologically, too, the results can be damaging. "The spiritual travail I passed through," says an English Roman Catholic mother of seven who decided to use contraceptives, "must also be the lot of my Catholic neighbours, but they suffer in silence from a terrible guilt from which they have no relief."[30] "One close friend," writes an American Catholic mother,

had had virtually no success with the rhythm method. I can scarcely forget the look of desperation in her eyes when she said, "I don't know what I can do. I just threw the thermometer away when I found I was pregnant again. This is our sixth child in seven years, and every one has to come by Cesarian section. I just don't know how much more I can take." . . . Whenever the period is late . . . there is a time of panic. I know of husbands who have exploded in helpless rage and wives who have become hysterical under these circumstances.[31]

Those are eloquent words, but conservative moralists in the Church, though they profess sympathy, have made little effort to explore the possibilities of theological solutions to such problems. Michael Novak has therefore written:

Perhaps the most grievous moral harm which laymen suffer in marriage questions is that of an enforced dishonesty. . . . These persons are faced with the dilemma either of accepting on authority what they do not accept in their own mind, or of following their own conscience despite an authority they have all their lives respected and obeyed. Very little in Catholic training prepares them for such a dilemma.[32]

This is a point that the Church has too often neglected. Father McCormack's talk about "moral dynamite," for instance, tends to equate "immorality" solely with sex. Sexual immorality has come to be an abiding preoccupation with many people in our society, but we ought to remember that nine of the Ten Commandments have nothing to do with sex. I believe that the absence of birth control ultimately destroys more moral integrity and accounts for more bad behavior than contraceptives could ever cause. "What is this morality," asks Ambassador Chagla, "which condemns millions of children to poverty and destitution? . . . I think it is better not to be born than to be born to live a life where there is no human dignity."[33]

"Through poverty many have sinned," says Ecclesiasticus, and Pope Pius XII once remarked that "sufferings [often] increase the state of weakness and physical exhaustion, check the ardor of the soul, and sap the moral powers instead of sustaining them."[34] In a shocking sociological study of underdeveloped Sicily, Danilo Dolci translates this papal principle into the language of the human beings he interviewed:

A mother, on All Souls' Day:

" 'Why can't I have some new shoes, Mommy?' he asked me.

" 'Because I haven't got any money,' I said, and he burst into tears. He went on and on till I lost my temper and smacked him. I wish I hadn't; it makes me feel terrible. That's him out in the street . . ."

The six-year-old who's just been smacked, red with rage, yells at his mother: "Go to hell! Go to hell the whole lousy bunch of you!"[35]

"Respondent No. 42" answers the question, "Do you think it is God's will that you are unemployed?"

Don't talk to me about God! When my mind's at peace, I believe in Him and His saints. I believe there was one Supreme Being, and so on. But when a man can't find work, he's filled with a black rage. I feel as though there were a wheel in my brain which keeps on missing a turn—it drives me into screaming out: "F . . . the lot of you!" to God and all his saints.[36]

And these unfortunate people, it should be noted, are Roman Catholics.

Children who are recklessly rather than responsibly bred frequently find themselves in a hostile, merciless world. (Needy South Koreans, in the first eight months of 1962, *abandoned* eight hundred infants in the city of Seoul alone.[37]) Ironically, if the bodies of such children are miserable in this life, as they are almost certain to be, then it is statistically more probable that their accompanying souls will be warped with immorality, and therefore (according to traditional Christian principles) condemned to an eternal hell in the next life. "Sufficient grace" is supposed to prevent such unjust results, but that doctrine does not square with statistics from the criminal courts.

I once spent a day in New York observing such a court. I watched trials involving various kinds of sordid crimes, and then talked with a lawyer attached to the court. What kind of people were these criminals? The lawyer's answer was prompt, and was what one might have expected: "For the most part, these are the people who don't have a fair share of the things of this world." This sounded very much like Tara Ali Baig's remark in New Delhi: "Desperation and insecurity become, for a [slum] family . . . a second nature, blighting their entire lives."[38] If we are really concerned about morality, we must take an interest not only in sexual improprieties but also in the deep and sinuous roots of envy, covetousness, resentment, bitterness, and desperation. These are fertilized by poverty—and poverty becomes inevitable whenever expanding populations outstrip the supply of the "things of this world."

When Religion Becomes Politics

> Catholics are bound in conscience to exercise civil and religious tolerance and to respect the constitutional rights of others.
> —REV. JOHN A. O'BRIEN[39]

Moral and religious choices must be free choices. Some Catholic thinkers recognize this; the Reverend Stanislas de Lestapis, a Jesuit professor of sociology with whom I talked in Paris, cites a statement of the Archbishop of Bologna: "Respect for truth demands liberty of consent: a truth imposed is a truth which is not accepted as such . . . *In the case of imposition of truth, there is a confusion between religion and politics . . .*"[40]

Not all Catholic thinkers are so clear-headed on this subject, however. The *Catholic Dictionary*, for instance, defines "freedom of worship" as "the inalienable right of all men to worship God *according to the teaching of the Catholic Church.*"[41] And the *Catholic Almanac* defines "freedom of thought" in this way: "Liberty to think the truth. In our day the expression has come to mean liberty to think as one pleases; this is an error. Our rational nature demands that we think only the truth, whatever the impact of outside forces or our own appetites."[42] A standard American Catholic textbook on politics makes a similar point. Discussing "liberalism," it states that "The fundamental principle of . . . liberalism is absolute freedom of thought, speech, press, politics, conscience and religion. . . . It . . . exalts the 'sovereignty of the people' as unrestrained and absolute." All of which sounds familiarly and pleasantly American. However, the authors go on to say, such liberalism "has been severely condemned by several of the Popes" and "this species of liberalism cannot be accepted by any Catholic who is at once loyal to his Church and adequately instructed."[43]

Acting on such principles, the Catholic Church (like other churches, but more concertedly) has traditionally used its influence to enact its own sectarian beliefs into laws carrying penalties for non-Catholics as well as for Catholics, and to obstruct legislation which it disapproves, even though Catholics would not themselves be adversely affected by it. The Church, said Pope Pius XI, "never can relinquish her God-given task of interposing her authority . . . in all those matters that have a bearing on moral conduct."[44]

Birth control is considered one such matter. In the United States, where only one-fourth of the population is Catholic, public opinion is heavily in favor of birth control. Both a 1959 Gallup Poll and a 1960 *New York Herald Tribune* poll found 72 per cent of those interviewed in favor of making birth control information available to anyone who wanted it. A recent *San Francisco Chronicle* poll found 83 per cent in favor, and a 1963 Gallup Poll reported 74 per cent in favor.

Despite this consistently overwhelming public sentiment,

however, the Catholic Church has repeatedly used its influence to impose its notions on the general public, thus confusing religion with politics. Father John A. O'Brien has deplored Catholics' "occasional resort to the police power of the state to suppress contraceptive birth control practices."[45] But prior restraints are equally disturbing; the District of Columbia is a useful microcosm. For years District Commissioners have been trying to obtain funds for birth control services to needy families. At one point this proposal was blocked by a Catholic member of the House Appropriations Subcommittee, which authorizes the District budget.[46] Thus the moral and economic decisions of many thousands of persons in our national capital were preempted by one man. Not until 1963 were funds finally made available for birth control devices and information.

Political pressure was used in New York in 1964, where the New York State Catholic Welfare Committee attacked a new program to offer birth control to welfare recipients, even though Catholics were not required to participate. And it revealed itself a year earlier in Illinois. Two-thirds of the patients at the Cook County Hospital in Chicago are non-Catholic, and the birth rate among the poorer ones is almost as high as that in India. Yet the hospital staff has always been forbidden to mention birth control to the patients. When a state commission proposed to change this rule, there was a protest from Catholics and subsequently the outspoken chairman of the commission was dismissed. The *New York Times* editorialized that the chairman's advocacy of birth control "was the real basis for his ouster."[47]

On the national level, Catholic political influence is particularly effective. In the early days of the Kennedy Administration, the policy-planning staff of the State Department, apparently worried about the population explosion, authorized an investigation of it. A report by the National Institutes of Health, completed in 1961, was suppressed because it would have led to "misunderstanding." However, it was decided to release a revised version by the end of 1962, after it had been "thoroughly reviewed."[48] Apparently the original report carried a recommendation that the U.S. government finance more research into new methods of fertility control—a recommendation that was later deleted.

A similar acute sensitiveness to Catholic influence appeared when, in 1964, it was suggested in Congress that an anti-poverty bill might include birth control projects. The sponsors of the bill angrily retorted that the suggestion was "fantastic" and "improper."[49]

Catholic opposition to birth control is not limited to direct influence on local, state, and national governments. It also operates powerfully in the business community. In 1961, the Ortho Pharmaceutical Corporation decided to advertise contraceptive products. It took contracts with five national women's magazines and ran a singularly subtle advertisement: two women talking over a fence, with the caption, "Don't plan your family over the back fence." This quiet exhortation produced the familiar protests from Catholic readers and was greeted by the Catholic periodical *America* with the words: "It was only a matter of time, of course. But now it is happening. . . . [The advertisement] is highly significant. *It indicates a willingness to risk public outcry from Catholics.*"[50] At once the manufacturer withdrew the advertisements.

Pressure is exerted by Catholics in other nations, too. Henri Fabre, a gynecologist in Grenoble, France, reported the opening of a family planning center in that predominantly Catholic country. Once the center was opened, he wrote in 1962, Catholic spokesmen asked the public authorities:

1. To shut it down immediately, with penalties against the promoters;
2. To legalize contraceptive methods permitted by them and prohibit other methods;
3. To make taxpayers' money available for the support of centers run on the lines advocated by the Roman Catholic Church.[51]

Throughout Latin America, too, politicians feel compelled to ignore their extremely fast, economically debilitating population growth because of Church opposition to fertility control. In heavily Catholic Puerto Rico, where Governor Muñoz Marin had advocated birth control as part of the country's economic planning, local Catholic bishops officially opposed his re-election, declaring it a sin to vote for him. He was elected anyway, but later his government, apparently out of deference to Catholic wishes, restricted the program of the family planning association.[52] In Canada, where politicians keep a watchful eye on Catholic Quebec, it is illegal to prescribe or sell birth control devices. In Korea, Barbara Cadbury writes, when the Minister of Health mentioned family planning in a public speech, he was immediately visited by American Catholic missionaries who said that "such policies, by offending American Catholic voters, might prejudice aid to Korea and might make it difficult to collect money for Korean charities in the United States." She also had reports of similar warnings in Formosa.[53]

International organizations have been subject to similar pressures. As long ago as 1951, India requested technical aid from the United Nations to establish its national family planning program. The U.N. World Health Organization sent a special mission on that occasion to experiment with the rhythm method (which was a significant failure); but ever since, Catholic-influenced nations have effectively banned even this sort of U.N. action. In 1961, during a U.N. General Assembly debate on birth control, Argentina's ambassador declared that his government was "categorically opposed" to the adoption of the principles of birth control by the U.N.; later the Vatican praised this statement as "a noble document."[54] Again in 1962, Catholic Argentina, France, and Peru were largely responsible for deleting from a U.N. declaration a proposal for technical assistance on population control. Brock Chisholm, former director of the World Health Organization, wrote in 1960,

No person can get anywhere in any agency of the United Nations who tries to talk frankly about population problems. . . . Every committee is under the influence of the Roman Catholic Church, and no delegate from the United States, Canada, France, Britain, and many other countries of Europe is in a position to defy that taboo.[55]

Thus Catholic influence has so far prevented both the United States government and the United Nations from significantly assisting underdeveloped countries with their population problems—even though high officials in some of those countries have urgently requested our aid. (Opponents of birth control have proposed that other peoples would "resent" our helping them with population control, but in fact the reverse is true: they resent our *refusing* to help.) The leaders of both India and Pakistan have informally requested aid: in both countries Catholics constitute less than one per cent of the population. But our government, far from being able to give effective aid, has hardly begun its homework on the problem. The subject of birth control, then, is clearly one of those matters over which religion has become confused with politics. Nor is it very democratic politics. Roman Catholics, who constitute at most only 15 per cent of the world's population, are, by their influence upon Western governments, holding a veto power over the moral and economic choice of vast numbers of non-Catholics around the world. For the hundreds of millions of people who are thus, in effect, disfranchised, this comes close to qualifying as a kind of dictatorship.

Catholic Conservatives and Catholic Power

> It is a strange desire to seek power and to lose liberty.
>
> —FRANCIS BACON[56]

Another instance of conservative thinking among Catholics is the attitude of some of them toward expansion. Catholics who tend to confuse religion with politics sometimes give the impression that the Roman Catholic Church forbids birth control to its own members simply in order to increase its following and therefore its temporal power. This is unfortunate, for—as one Catholic, Norman St. John-Stevas, writes—"when Protestants visualize the Church, the image will not be that of a religious body, but of a political power structure."[57] The editor of the Catholic lay journal *Commonweal* repeated this charge in 1963, adding, "To some extent this image is due to . . . prejudice, but to some extent too I think we have helped to bring it on ourselves."[58] Nevertheless, some Catholics go on emphasizing the growth of temporal influence rather than the spread of Catholic faith. The journal of the Holy Name Society reported in 1960, for instance, that "Unless there are some surprising changes in birth rates or marked shifts in immigration policy—neither likely —sooner or later Catholics will be the numerically dominating group of citizens in the United States."[59] Various Catholic officials have emphasized this point,[60] and a pamphlet issued by the Catholic Truth Society in London makes its satisfaction at such trends explicit: "Our faithful Catholic mothers are doing a wonderful work for God. In time, if contraceptive practices continue to prevail amongst Protestants, their number will decrease and the Catholic race will prevail, and thus England might again become what it once was, a Catholic country."[61] Such statements, hinging on words like "dominating" and "prevail," give the impression that some Catholics see offspring as political rather than spiritual assets.

The Roman Catholic Church, like any highly organized, centralized institution, is, of course, a type of power structure, and such structures seem to have a strong inherent tendency toward expansion. Perhaps this partly accounts for some Catholics' politically-oriented remarks about population growth. A few weeks before I visited Warsaw, Cardinal Wyszinski struck out at abortions in Poland on the grounds that Poland must have more people to become a "great nation."[62] A recent letter to the editor of the Catholic periodical *America* noted that barbarians were able to conquer Rome because "for years Rome had lacked the manpower to defend its frontiers." And the writer went on to say, "We in the West had better get over some of our foolish notions [about birth control], or we will one day find ourselves eating with chopsticks." *America* then editorialized against "unilateral depopulation."[63] In the near background of such political remarks always lies that suggestion of a potential breeding contest. Ironically, though, because they have blocked birth control assistance to foreign nations, Catholics are partly responsible for the high Asian growth rates—and therefore partly responsible for the fact that Catholics are daily becoming a smaller and smaller fraction of the world's population.

Catholic Conservatives and the Language of Bad Will

Partisanship warps truth.
—CARL BECKER[64]

Today many of those concerned about population expansion, both Catholic and non-Catholic, are calling for the understanding and cooperation of all men of good will to meet the emergency. This is an obviously well-intentioned thought; yet conservative Catholics, by their words as well as their deeds, are obstructing such cooperation.

It is only fair to point out that this obstructionism is motivated by conscience; after all, traditional Catholic beliefs and convictions are deeply involved. Unfortunately, the old taboo on birth control is so powerful that some Catholics still cannot think about it without responding emotionally, in harsh, even violent language. An English Catholic attacks arguments for birth control, for instance, as "insidious vaporings" full of "stock-yard phraseology."[65] A French priest calls them "infantile,"[66] and American priests refer to them as "perverted,"[67] "lewd," "obscene,"[68] and the work of "fellow travelers of the communists";[69] government-sponsored research in birth control, insists one American priest, would be "subsidizing fornication and adultery."[70] Cardinal Wyszinski, preaching to his flock in 1963, condemned birth control as "murder" and declared that the hands of family planning workers are "stained with the blood of infants."[71] In 1964 he compared a government-sponsored birth control program to Nazi genocide.[72] The Vatican newspaper calls birth control information "propagandistic licentiousness,"[73] and a Catholic pamphlet series reprints a Belgian Cardinal's words about "ruffians" who spread "filthy literature," "dastardly propaganda," and "rotten, unwholesome ideas" in a "vile campaign" for birth control.[74]

Such phraseology is hardly the language of good will, but this is more than just a question of good manners. It is a serious tactical question, too, for those who hope for an eventual accommodation between Catholics and non-Catholics on this subject. How long will the advocates of birth control be content to turn a soft answer to such open wrath? How long can the Church expect to be treated with respect while using the language of bad will? One fears that this language may further alienate the participants in this controversy. "Among wolves," Voltaire reflected, "one must howl a little."

An Essay on Development

> Out of the living Church . . . come new applications of the truths of faith . . . The alternative to this kind of change is stagnation and spiritual exhaustion.
> —RICHARD CARDINAL CUSHING[75]

I should not close this chapter with the impression that I think conservative Catholics are always wrong or always irresponsible. It is an unfortunate habit of our time to assume that any challenge to a religious position must be due to bigotry. Not at all; I respect a man's right to any religious doctrine he chooses to hold, however mistaken I may personally consider it. But some mistakes are purely personal and therefore socially harmless, whereas others are public and therefore socially malignant. The Catholics' great mistake about birth control is, I think, one of the latter, and it ought to be debated.

By an unhappy paradox, it is not the old superstitions of ignorant people in isolated straw-hut villages that are blocking birth control and thus hampering economic development. The hindrance that must be dealt with is an idea promoted by the world's best organized and most sophisticated theological institution, acting upon and through the agencies of the wealthiest and most literate nations of the world.

"The Church," writes one Catholic spokesman, "even if she wished, could no more permit birth prevention than she could permit blasphemy"[76]—yet in the Middle Ages, Churchmen said similar things about taking interest for the loan of money; later the Church decided that it was only certain rates of interest that were evil and not others. Some such decision is overdue on the subject of birth control. The Roman Catholic Church is not, in theory, opposed to the development and reinterpretation of its ideas, though this is always slow work. It is, it seems to me, the obligation of theologians to keep religious doctrines in touch with the facts of life; so far this has not been accomplished with respect to birth control. That is why the population problem is, for people in the West, a Catholic problem. It concerns all of us to some degree, but it concerns particularly those powerful conservatives in the Roman hierarchy who wield great influence over the consciences of millions of rank-and-file Catholics but who fail to invest this sacred trust with the responsible working of an informed and critical intelligence—and who therefore lose contact with the real world and betray that trust.

Pope John XXIII's summoning of the Second Vatican Council, after all, was a call for "aggiornamento"—for an updating, a revitalizing of the Church. It is a hopeful sign that participants in the Council have vigorously discussed birth control teachings. Cardinal Suenens, the Archbishop of Malines-Brussels, calling the issue "one of the major contemporary problems" of Catholicism, has urged the Council to reassess the traditional position on birth control. To do so, however, the liberals will have to overcome powerful conservative forces at the Council— something they were apparently not able to do in its first sessions.[77] Even some of the more perceptive Catholic spokesmen resist all talk of change. The Jesuit periodical *America* commented in 1963: "The trial balloons which are periodically sent up suggesting that the Church is about to change her doctrine on the immorality of artificial contraception are wasted effort. The Church is not about to do any such thing."[78]

The need for vigorous public discussion of this subject therefore continues. There is great social value in controversy: in debates, letters to editors, petitions, picketing, and non-violent public demonstrations of all kinds; for these are signs of legitimate attention to social problems that are otherwise all too often suffered in silence by the victims and all too easily and comfortably forgotten by the rest of us. We are all conservatives on a full stomach, as Emerson said, and American stomachs are almost always full. We therefore sometimes avoid looking at problems until they explode directly under us. Instead, we cultivate clichés like "Agitation isn't going to help things," or "You can't legislate morality," or "We should wait for a change in the minds and hearts of men"—forgetting that few great and worthwhile social changes ever came about without agitation; forgetting that we can and do legislate upon the morality of murder, theft, rape, false witness, and so on; and forgetting that the minds and hearts of most men are the last things to change in most societies and must always be led to change by the alert intelligence, the thoughtfulness, and the agitation of that saving remnant in the community that refuses to lapse into conservatism, even after dinner. Until the Catholic hierarchy becomes as perceptive about birth control as it has been about usury, then, the need for controversy will continue. Meanwhile, the well-intentioned inflexibility of conservative Roman Catholics will continue to bear a heavy part of the responsibility for the crushing misery of millions of their fellow human beings.

Chapter 5

Ideology and the Liberals: Changing the Changeless

> *If our church were afraid to change, Galileo would still be wrong, Joan would certainly be no saint, and a new crop of Inquisitors would still be burning the heretics—and the faithful—at the stake.*
>
> —DOMINICAN PRIEST[1]

On Lenin's ninety-third birthday, I heard a Soviet historian deliver a panegyric on Lenin's virtues. Praise of Lenin in the Soviet Union is apt to be remarkably fulsome; the cult of personality, now that it has lost Stalin as an object, centers on Lenin: he is father, prophet, savior, and patron saint, in one. This is characteristic of authoritarian ideologies. The mantle of infallibility cannot exist in a vacuum; it must be draped around some specific figure. No peasant was ever inspired to good works by the image of a committee.

Once the mantle is well adjusted, it becomes a permanent fixture. (Khrushchev tore it from Stalin in the nick of time, and *his* successors began de-Khrushchevizing immediately.) The saints of an authoritarian ideology *must* be right; that is what it means to be a saint. Therefore, new ideas about Communist theory must pose, preferably under the imprimatur (however inappropriate) of the prophet, Lenin, as "concrete instances" in which "the science of Marxism" is revealing the truth about the world. Similarly, new ideas in a dogmatic Church must be seen as new developments of Eternal Truth. (I hope it is clear that I am comparing only ideological tactics now, not the aims or spirit of communism and Catholicism.)

An ideology is, after all, an institutionalized way of thinking

about life. It is convenient because it permits instant responses
to problems. Of course these responses may be right—that is, the
best possible ones for a given situation. The difficulties arise when
they are wrong, but are nevertheless inflexible. Then a whole
society may develop a sort of ideological schizophrenia, a serious
split between what the prevailing ideology insists is right and
what people's sense or senses tell them is right.

When such a condition arises in decentralized societies
where ideology is not officially imposed or where there is even
some serious disagreement about what the prevailing ideology
is or ought to be, the split can be mended by changing or adapt-
ing the ideology in whatever way seems necessary. (This is what
has happened in the West, to take an obvious instance, to laissez-
faire economics, under the impact of changing social conditions
and newer—especially Keynesian—theories.)

But if the ideology is the basis of an authoritarian system,
it cannot be so easily changed or discarded, and schizophrenia
may set in. Attempts to remake the world so that it will fit an
old ideology are rarely successful; history does not repeat itself
that obligingly. Authority is therefore called upon to be more
and more insistent and less and less reasonable—and usually ends
by looking ridiculous. That is what happened when the flat-
earthers and geocentrists of the Catholic Church persecuted
Galileo. It has happened more recently in the U.S.S.R., in the
notorious ideological perversion of the science of genetics.

This case I take to be well known, but a quick résumé will
help to demonstrate the authoritarian pattern. Mendelian genetics,
the Soviets have insisted, is based on a mistaken bourgeois theory.
By its stress on inherited qualities and abilities, it could tend
to undermine egalitarianism, to discourage Soviet attempts to
improve upon human nature by changing man's economic and
social environment, and, finally, to decrease the emphasis on
class struggle. Therefore Soviet scientists had to invent a new,
ideologically acceptable genetics. The accommodating scientist
who did so won Stalin's quick approval; dissenting scientists were
then liquidated, books were burned, and laboratories were closed.
In the face of such determined action, even the reluctant scientists capitulated: "I, as a party member," one of them vowed, "do
not consider it possible to retain the views which have been

recognized as erroneous by the Central Committee of our party."[2] (To realize the enormity of such a statement, we would have to envision Einstein scrapping $E = mc^2$ on orders from Washington.) So today (although the post-Stalin thaw may now be slowly changing this as well as other things), the Soviet Union is stuck with a "science" which is undemonstrable outside its own laboratories and would be—if it were not so deplorable—the laughingstock of the rest of the scientific world.

Authoritarian ideologies, then, begin with the twin assumptions that the Truth is known to them, and that—in a very practical way—no error is harmless. That is why my Soviet hosts, who clearly wanted to be friendly and who spoke warmly of peaceful coexistence, nevertheless constantly reiterated: "There can be *no* coexistence in ideology"; that is the most-repeated single sentence I heard in the Soviet Union. And the same assumptions account for statements such as this by Roman Catholic theologians: "When the Church defines a doctrine she . . . declares infallibly that this belief is part of the *original* revelation . . ." and "The heretic is one who even after the Church has spoken . . . contumaciously defends his error."[3]

Despite this straining after certainty, however, both Catholic church and Communist state have, when necessary, acknowledged that a shifting world requires re-examinations and redefinitions. Recently there have been an increasing number of hopeful signs that both parties are taking a fresh look at their positions on overpopulation and birth control.

Types of Flexibility: Communist Liberals

> Capitalism is the exploitation of man by man; Communism is the opposite.
> —JOKE CIRCULATING IN WARSAW IN 1963

The emergence of a sardonic analytical humor in Eastern Europe is one of many indications that even a monolithic power structure backed by an authoritarian ideology cannot always enforce strict uniformity of opinion. Since Stalin's demise, Communist thinkers have shown a remarkable willingness to explore new ideas and attitudes. As one result of this ferment, the strict Marxist line on overpopulation has been gradually breaking down. (Not in theory, of course; only in fact: that is the secret of changing an ideology; later any discrepancies can be explained by making perceptive distinctions.) After World War II, all of the Eastern European nations were pro-natalist. Today only hard-line Albania and depopulated East Germany (a special case, partly because of rapid emigration) remain so.

Poland offers a useful case study because it is both strongly Catholic and Communist. By every reasonable expectation, then, it should also be strongly opposed to birth control, as in fact it was until recently. For a decade after the war, the theme of "building a strong nation," coupled with a general party-line disparagement of the fear of overpopulation, caused the birth rate to rise. Then the planners began to have doubts. The housing situation was bad, partly because of war damage—and it remained bad, despite their efforts. Food supplies had never been bountiful, and they remained scanty, despite planners' efforts. A decade after the war, an impatient people were demanding better living conditions. The planners, who preferred capital investments to the production of consumer goods for a multiplying people, finally realized that rapid population growth was a serious problem.

In 1957 the Polish government took the un-communistic step of establishing a Polish planned parenthood association. The director of the association in 1963 was a stocky, voluble woman; she spoke to me at high speed for over an hour about their activities. The association has its own clinics in Warsaw and Krakow as well as 1,200 others in the community clinics of the Ministry of Health; besides this, trained doctors are visiting the smaller towns and villages. The association advertises its services in newspapers and magazines, on radio and television, and by leaflets and booklets in the hundreds of thousands (to an aggregate of more than ten million) distributed through social organizations and labor unions. Thus there is a great deal of new awareness of the subject and this is reflected in the increasing sales of contraceptives, which run in the tens of millions per year. The director spoke of all this with obvious pride, tempered with the warning that much remained to be done.

How do the Poles reconcile all this with Communist anti-Malthusianism? First of all, East European demographers are now conceding that "a form of overpopulation may, *at times and under certain conditions,* exist in a communist society."[4] Does this mean that the Communists are finally making concessions to the Malthusians? Not at all, because (as the important Polish newspaper, *Zycie Warszawy,* explains):

Our population policy springs on the one hand from an analysis of reality and on the other hand from the principles of lay humanism. Even if one or two of its elements may be compared to certain conclusions of Malthus, it should be stated that even the most inveterate ideological opponents agree on the thesis that two and two make four.[5]

To understand this explanation, you have to recognize "dialectical" thinking. Arthur Koestler gave an instructive example of it in *The God That Failed.* Marx had written in the *Communist Manifesto* that "The bourgeois family will vanish as a matter of course with the vanishing of Capital" and he dismisses "bourgeois claptrap" about "the haloed correlation of parent and child." But a difficulty developed in actual practice:

Bourgeois morality was a Bad Thing. But promiscuity was an equally Bad Thing, and the only correct, concrete attitude towards the sexual urge was Proletarian Morality. This consisted in getting married, being faithful to one's spouse, and producing proletarian babies. But then, was this not the same thing as bourgeois morality?—The question, Comrade, shows that you are thinking in mechanistic, not in dialectical, terms . . . The institution of marriage which in capitalist society is an aspect of bourgeois decay, is dialectically transformed in its function in a healthy proletarian society. Have you understood, Comrade . . . ?[6]

It is this kind of thinking that permits the new approach to birth control and overpopulation. "*Our* emphasis on family planning," Chou told Edgar Snow, "is entirely positive; planned parenthood, where there is increased production of goods and services, is conducive to raising the people's standard of living."[7] In the course of a long conversation in Moscow with a young Soviet economist, a specialist in the economy of India, I found it easy to elicit agreement on the issue of overpopulation. While overtly holding to the traditional Marxist position, he also agreed that in the underdeveloped countries, "there is a necessity to limit population growth." Such thinking is beginning to be reflected in more complex attitudes among Soviet delegates to international organizations. In the 1962 U.N. General Assembly debate on population growth, Communist-bloc delegates held to the traditional anti-Malthusian position, but when the vote came on a positive resolution, the Soviet bloc did not oppose it but merely abstained.[8]

The Communist position is evolving, then, and has evolved, at this point, further than that of the Catholics. In Poland this has led to a head-on clash, with Cardinal Wyszinski lashing at the government for promoting birth control, and the government replying caustically. The Church has asserted that Poland could support eighty million people. (The present population is about thirty million.) Secretary Gomulka replied in 1960:

Should church dignitaries find such miraculous means with the aid of which we should be able to attain . . . the industrial production to support this population increase . . . we too shall become ardent propagators . . . of the goal . . . of an 80 million nation. The fact is, however, that miracles do not happen, and that church dignitaries are leaving to us the concern for the life of the nation while they remain free of this responsibility.[9]

I recently published an article on overpopulation in a national magazine.[10] In the resulting correspondence, I heard from a Polish graduate student now in this country: "Cardinal Wyszinski and his bishops," he wrote, "were fighting the government . . . for its tendency to establish population control on a voluntary basis. The Church was so bitterly opposed to any [birth] control that it finally lost out completely. People could not afford big families, so they turned from the Church to the state for help."

This "turn from the Church to the state" has been serious enough to alarm many Polish priests. "Our opposition," the director of the Polish planned parenthood group told me, "comes from the higher Church authorities, not from the village priests." One Polish priest wrote in 1960:

I personally cannot agree with the view of the Roman Church. . . . Contraceptives . . . are not something evil and sinful. . . . If the parents already have, say three children, and cannot have more for one or another reason, then they should resort with an easy conscience to either sexual abstinence or contraceptives."[11]

Types of Flexibility: The Revolt of the Roman Catholic Laity

> My husband is a strict Catholic, but he wants to be a good father to the ones he's got. He even told the priest that. He said he'd have as many kids as the priest wanted if the priest sent him a check every month. The priest had a fit. We both confess it and have to make a penance for it.
>
> —CATHOLIC MOTHER IN A CHICAGO SLUM[12]

Poland is not the only country where there has been a "turn from the Church" because of birth control. Throughout Catholic Europe, birth rates are now lower than in the predominantly Protestant United States,[13] and similar reports are emerging from other Catholic countries. In Trinidad, three-fourths of the Christian patients at a new family planning clinic were Catholics.[14] In Jamaica a survey has found that Catholic parents in the sample have smaller families than non-Catholics, know more about birth control, and use it more than Protestants.[15] In strongly Catholic Puerto Rico, Muñoz Marin, who favors birth control, was re-elected governor despite strong opposition by members of the Catholic hierarchy there.[16]

In the United States, too, this revolt is in progress. A poll by the Planned Parenthood Federation of America in 1960 showed that a majority of Catholic lay leaders favored non-Catholics' "freedom of conscience and action concerning birth control."[17] A 1963 Gallup Poll found almost half of the Catholics polled favoring the free availability of birth control information in the United States and elsewhere.

Furthermore, American Catholics not only favor non-Catholics' freedom to use contraceptives; they are using them increasingly themselves. A national survey in 1955 revealed that half of all fertile Catholic couples married at least ten years had used "a method of family planning prohibited by the Church."[18] A Louis Harris survey in 1964 showed 49 per cent of Catholics in favor of changing the church's prohibition of birth control and only 32 per cent against such a change. A number of reasons were given for favoring change; in the terse survey reports they came out sounding rather impersonal: "Can't provide for child's needs," "Family too big now," and so forth.[19] Here, in more detail, are two American Catholic mothers' responses to a recent sociological survey in a slum area:

If I were trying to be sure not to conceive, the button would be the best for me and I would not hesitate to go and have one fitted. I am Catholic and I should not think this way, but you see too much in a neighborhood like this to think any other way.[20]

I am convinced that the real safe way is to be tied and I am going to have my doctor do the job. I am not going to say anything to the priest. Who is he to tell me about how many children to have? He never has to drag about with five kids and try to make a living for them! The way things are it just goes on making me old and cross and sick![21]

That is the eloquence of the poor.

Types of Flexibility: Catholic Intellectuals

> The Catholic moral consensus has
> also undergone a shift. . . . What
> appeared self-evident even a decade
> or so ago may now appear problem-
> atical.
>
> —EDITORIAL IN *Commonweal*[22]

The importance of Catholic social action has been emphasized again and again in the seventy years since Pope Leo
XIII's notable encyclical, *de Rerum novarum*, and it was given
added force and clarity in Pope John XXIII's *Mater et magistra*.
Nevertheless, when Catholic spokesmen have discussed the problem of feeding a multiplying world, they have in the past often
tended to concentrate on short-term, partial, or simplistic solutions to what are in fact long-term, complex problems. One
Catholic writer insisted flatly that "To pretend that God has not
given us enough earth to shelter, clothe, and feed all those who
should come into the world, is to cast aspersions on his infinite
Wisdom and infallible Providence."[23] Another advised grandly
that the Sahara should be "made to bloom," that we should eliminate "greed, selfishness, and ignorance."[24] Yet another put his
trust in an old saying: "Every child is born with a loaf of bread
under its arm."[25] Such proposals share, in one way or another,
the tranquilizing confidence of the Communists and the Cornucopians, that a favorable balance of resources-to-population can
be maintained despite explosive population growth.

Some Catholics, recognizing population growth to be a
genuine and formidable problem, have turned their attention to
population limitation; but again, until recently, their proposals
have tended to be unrealistic. One suggested raising the age of
marriage in Asia.[26] (This is being tried in Egypt, where the law
has established a sixteen-year minimum age for marriage; but,
a demographer there told me, poor people simply don't observe

the law—if necessary, they forge birth certificates.) Other Catholic thinkers have hoped to develop in the non-Christian peasant populations of the underdeveloped countries a Christian sense of "will," of "self-control," of a "deep and abiding asceticism," an "interest in prayer and spiritual things," so as to make possible family limitation by the rhythm system.[27] How does one develop this kind of will and asceticism? In the words of another Catholic writer, you have to "control the fierce blasts of passion, to stem the wild torrent of desire; and from out this work there comes that power of powers and force of forces, the disciplined will."[28] It is reasonably safe to say that such discipline has not been generally developed anywhere in the world. To imagine it coming about in a country where people still inhabit a "primitive world of superstition and fable, unable to read the clock, to decipher the simplest written calculation, or to read a leaflet"[29] is simply visionary.

Recently there have been more encouraging signs among Catholic intellectuals. The Roman Catholic Church is a far-flung organization and it has its full share of brilliant minds. Many alert Catholics are now energetically casting about for ways of correcting the great mistake on birth control. It is impossible to read a publication like the Catholic lay journal *Commonweal* without being impressed with the awareness of its editors and many of its contributors. A *Commonweal* editorial asserted in 1962, for instance, that "Catholics have a special obligation [to the population problem] since it is the Catholic Church which has most steadfastly opposed the most common non-Catholic solution: a crash program of world population control by means of contraceptives. . . . There is no longer any excuse for Catholic indifference."[30] In the same year, William J. Nagle wrote in *Commonweal* that he found "somewhat puzzling the head-in-the-sand posture of Catholic moralists on this [birth control] question." He urged Catholic theologians to "take a more careful look at our natural law argument against contraceptives."[31]

The Catholic World has also published thoughtful discussions of the subject. A Yale political scientist, Bruce Martin Russett, wrote in its pages in 1962 that "The Church is in serious difficulty in a number of Latin American States; it would be folly for it to ignore one of its flock's most basic problems. . . .

Practically no serious work on cultural factors affecting the
readiness of various peoples to accept contraceptive techniques
has been done. . . . The work must be planned. It will not just
happen."[32]

The Jesuit publication *America* reports a challenging speech
by Dr. John Battenfeld to a Catholic group:

The speaker pointed out [that] "a chaos of disorder and immorality"
is inevitable unless "Catholics strain their energies to the utmost for
a just and Christian solution of these highly complex and difficult
problems [of overpopulation]." . . . It is *only* facing facts to admit that
the problem continues to baffle demographers who are searching for
a solution based on Christian moral principles.[33]

And in 1964, *America* carried an article by a professor of law
urging Catholics "to accept as tolerable the involvement of the
state in contraceptive birth control measures so long as government remains neutral in the choice of means."[34]

Roman Catholic intellectuals have not contented themselves
with words. Dr. John Rock, a Catholic, was one of the men who
developed the first commercial oral contraceptive, Enovid. He
has also written a book, *The Time Has Come*, which has served
the useful purpose of drawing a great deal of public attention to
this problem. In 1963, Catholic Georgetown University began a
center for research on population problems, the first work of
which will be aimed at the possible improvement of the rhythm
method, though the researchers hope to "foster research on the
whole range of questions connected with human population,
whether or not they have any particular connection with
Catholicism."[35]

The Catholic liberals, then, differ remarkably from those
Catholic conservatives who are unwilling even to admit that new
kinds of world problems exist—much less try to explore new
kinds of solutions. I submit that the liberal Catholics are realists
and that the conservative Catholics have in fact adopted a head-
in-the-sand attitude—and that it is therefore up to the liberals in
the Church to save the conservatives from the potentially disastrous results of their own rigid policies. Fortunately, the priest-
hood itself is well endowed with such liberals.

Types of Flexibility: The Liberal Clergy

> Pope John XXIII . . . pleaded with
> us to adapt the age-old theology of
> the Catholic Church to conditions
> as they are in the world today.
> —THE MOST REV. JOSEPH A. BURKE,
> LATE BISHOP OF BUFFALO[36]

So much stir among the Catholic laity and Catholic intellectuals need not make any theological difference; from the point of view of the Church hierarchy, it can simply mean that more and more people are "wrong." The Catholic Church is not, after all, a democratic institution, and unless the hierarchy is convinced of a truth, it is not, officially, a truth. "If anything shall appear white to our eyes which the Church has declared as black," Ignatius Loyola insisted, "we likewise must declare it black."[37] When the Catholic writer Dr. Herbert Doms suggested that the traditional terminology of "primary" and "secondary" ends of marriage be abandoned, his book received an ecclesiastical censure.[38] When the Catholic doctor John Rock proposed that Enovid be accepted by the Church as a licit form of birth control, his suggestion was received by some Catholic spokesmen with indignation.[39] Even a bishop, Joseph Burke, when he instituted a Catholic "rhythm clinic," seemed to be moving with great caution.[40] And a cardinal, Leo Suenens, when he proposed that scientists might develop a pill that Catholics could use in family planning, was indirectly reprimanded by the secretary of the powerful Congregation of the Holy Office for speaking out prematurely on a debated question.[41]

Whatever courage it takes, however, to try to "adapt" an "age-old theology," the attempt is being made. For one thing, liberal Catholics are now emphasizing the values of freedom for the individual and for the Church. Father Hans Küng, the stimulating young thinker from the University of Tübingen, writes:

"Every manifestation in the Church of lack of freedom, however harmless, however much under cover, whatever religious trappings it may have, contributes toward making the Church less believable in the eyes of the world. . . . Freedom in the Church always has to be won over and over again."[42]

Accordingly, the temptation for the Church to seek civil legislation to support its traditional ideas is being criticized by the clergy. "A church's civil right," wrote the late Gustav Weigel, a Jesuit,

goes beyond the confines of its own closed fellowship. Its members, singly or together, can urgently propose their specific vision of life and reality to the community at large. . . . However, the community wants such ideas proposed, not imposed. The republic will decide; it refuses to have decisions made for it . . . In our kind of democracy, neither in law nor in fact does the community give the Church the right to be the arbiter of the nation's ethics.[43]

Furthermore, new approaches to the role of the Catholic layman are being developed by the liberal clergy, who seem to be finding new voices, new programs, and new courage. Several issues in the second Vatican Ecumenical Council have reflected these new attitudes. American bishops led the drive for the increased use of vernacular languages in Church services and—more important—for a declaration of the importance of the Catholic laity in both secular and spiritual matters (contradicting the Catholic conservatives' traditional insistence that the laity have no special share in the apostolic mission of the Church). "The spirit of God is not confined to the hierarchy," a Canadian priest said at the Council; "The Holy Ghost operates in all members of the Church."[44] Upon this basis the role of the Pope is also being reappraised, with a growing insistence upon the "corporate" nature of Church authority—emphasizing the role of the clergy and the responsibility of the clergy to the laity. The liberals of Vatican II have even been critical of that guardian of traditionalism, the Holy Office (successor to the Inquisition) for being out of harmony with modern times, "a source of harm to the faithful and of scandal to those outside the Church."[45]

Against the backdrop of this intellectual ferment, the Catholic liberals' new thinking on birth control is highly significant.

For one thing, there has been a new stress on previously muted papal pronouncements—such as Pope Pius XI's statement that to beget so many offspring that they cannot be properly brought up and educated is morally reprehensible,[46] or Pius XII's reference to the population crisis as "agonizing" and his judgment that "medical, .eugenic, economic and social grounds" are sufficient reasons for regulation of births.[47]

One after another, liberal priests are underscoring these thoughts: Catholics "have been oversold on procreation," warns Jesuit Father William J. Gibbons, "and undereducated on the responsibilities it entails."[48] The Rev. John L. Thomas, another Jesuit, believes that "No country can long make reasonable provision for its population increases unless a good percentage of its couples take some effective steps to regulate family size."[49] Bishop William M. Bekkers holds birth regulation to be "a normal part of the total task of a married couple."[50]

Beyond this, many priests are urging active Catholic participation in research in reproductive physiology. Father John Knott of the National Catholic Welfare Conference has written:

Much good could come from such basic research. The fact that such information could be used for what we as Catholics would consider immoral purposes should not prevent us from supporting those who are seeking the truth. Rather, we as Catholics, should positively encourage all efforts which have as their goal the unlocking of nature's secrets. Ignorance is more to be feared than truth or even its misuse.[51]

Such insistent and increasingly numerous pleas have now obviously alerted the hierarchy, but the conservative wing has managed thus far to keep the Church from acting upon them. The Church "has to keep on condemning contraception," writes one priest, "because she still *sees it* as a violation of the Natural Law."[52] That is precisely the point—must the Church continue to see it that way? The Church has changed not only the way it saw heliocentricity and usury; it also accommodated its traditional Aristotelian views on biology to newer, post-Darwinian views; it accommodated its traditional opposition to birth control to the relatively new concept of rhythm; and it has always been resourceful at making distinctions that clear the way for adaptations of doctrine. "Virtual distinction," says the *Catholic Dictionary*, is the art of distinguishing between "diverse formalities because the thing which is really one can produce different effects . . ."[53] Thus there may be new ways of looking at older, less refined doctrines. One priest, an adviser at the Vatican Council, proposes that "The sexual experience and the possibility of procreation may not be separated in the marriage-*project*. . . . But this can say nothing about the individual marriage-*act*. . . . the total marriage-project may exclude no single essential meaning. A separate act may . . ."[54] And Dr. Rock quotes another priest as writing: "the frustration which is morally evil is the frustration *of the whole* and not merely *of the part*. . . . In the matter of sexual morality, it is not enough to condemn an action as wrong simply because it frustrates the natural purposes of the sexual faculty; an action is proved to be wrong only if it frustrates the nature of *man*."[55] These fascinating and potentially fruitful ideas make it clear that there is ample opportunity for distinctions and reinterpretations by Catholic theologians which might lead to rewarding new strategies in the struggle against overpopulation.

Will the Church do this kind of rethinking? A parable may be instructive. In 1885, A. D. White wrote:

Smallpox broke out with great virulence in Montreal. The Protestant population escaped almost entirely by vaccination; but multitudes of their Catholic fellow-citizens, under some vague survival of the old orthodox ideas, refused vaccination and suffered fearfully. . . . The Board of Health struggled against this superstition, and addressed a circular to the Catholic clergy, imploring them to recommend vaccination; but, though two or three complied with this request, the great majority were either silent or openly hostile.[56]

It is never comfortable to scrutinize one's own basic principles; the Catholic leaders of Montreal were, no doubt, sincerely and emotionally committed to the idea that vaccination was morally wrong. Yet, when it became clear, as the epidemic wore on, that the alternative to vaccination was disaster, they found it possible to correct this mistaken judgment. The present issue of population control dwarfs the issue of vaccination in a single city, but the moral is the same. It is high time for intelligence, ingenuity, and conscientious concern to bear upon the reinterpretation of this one aspect of natural law.

Natural law, according to Catholic doctrine, is supposed to be constant and unchanging. Yet the current interpretation of natural law, by obstructing research in and development of techniques of population regulation, makes the Church indirectly responsible for the growing problems attendant on overpopulation: responsible for incalculable pain, misery, and sorrow for hundreds of millions of people; responsible for envy, hatred, theft, and murder in millions more; and responsible for the slow death of hundreds of thousands of our fellow men—the innocent victims of theological intransigence. Catholic humanitarians are distressed by such misery and evil, but find it impossible to overcome by good works, however well-intentioned and skillful, the dismaying amount of misery now aggravated by overpopulation. Thus, in a ruthlessly fast-moving world, Catholic liberals are now pointing out that it is not enough to be a severe but ineffectual voice crying in the wilderness. To keep the respect of its own followers and gain the good will of others, to be a real "sign in the world," the Church must cease to be satisfied with obstructionism. It must, in realistic and effective ways, champion the cause of human betterment—even if this means reappraising its own teachings.

The Vatican Ecumenical Council

> Should this Council say nothing about the whole population explosion . . . it would create the impression that it stands outside the world.
> —PRIEST AT THE VATICAN COUNCIL[57]

Pope Paul VI announced in June, 1964, "It will be necessary to look carefully and squarely at this theoretical as well as practical development of the [birth control] question. And this is in fact what the Church is doing. The question is under study, a study as broad and deep as possible . . ."[58] The Pope was referring specifically to a papal commission which he had created, but the widespread Catholic interest in birth control was also apparent later at the third session of the Vatican Ecumenical Council. Catholic prelates there debated a schema on "The Church in the Modern World," which considered "the joys and griefs, and the hopes and the anxieties of modern man, especially of the poor and the afflicted." Significantly, this schema linked economic, demographic, and family problems, including a new look at Catholic teachings relating to the use of contraceptives.

Cardinal Suenens of Malines-Brussels, who had originally proposed this schema, assured the bishops at the Council in October, 1964, that there would be nothing to fear in making a thorough inquiry into Church teachings on birth control: "Modern science may well have much to tell us," he said. Cardinal Suenens was immediately supported by a number of influential prelates. Cardinal Léger of Montreal questioned the traditional Catholic position that procreation is the primary end of marriage. Maximos IV Saigh, Melchite Patriarch of Antioch, flatly proposed that "the official position of the Church on this matter should be revised on the basis of modern theological, medical, psychological, and sociological science." These men apparently represented the majority opinion of the Council; Cardinal Suenens was reported to have received the most thunderous applause of the session.[59]

The conservative prelates, however, stubbornly opposed all suggested innovations in birth control doctrine; they did not want the subject even to be discussed. Cardinal Ruffini of Palermo insisted that the rhythm method was "everything we need" and that discussion of any other method of birth limitation was superfluous. "Can it be possible," asked Cardinal Ottaviani, secretary of the powerful and conservative Holy Office, "that the Church has erred for centuries?"[60] Because of this and other attempts to update Church teachings, the conservatives even attempted to end the Council prematurely with the third session or, failing that, to delay the fourth, and presumably decisive, session for an inordinately long period.[61]

Because of the technical scientific and medical problems involved, the Council will almost certainly not come to a decision on this sensitive subject until the papal commission makes its recommendations and the Pope himself pronounces upon it. There has been no indication of how long this will take, but it seems reasonable to expect a report sometime between the third and fourth sessions of the Council, so that the prelates of the fourth session could discuss the schema again, bring it to final debate, and vote on it.

The unanswerable question at this writing is: what position will the papal commission and the Pope take? Will their investigations be broad and bold enough, their conclusions genuinely constructive? "As of now," Pope Paul warned in 1964, "we do not have sufficient reason to regard the norms [of conduct on birth control] given by Pope Pius XII as surpassed . . ."[62] And the discussion of birth control in the third session of the Council, though it displeased Council conservatives, was not exactly daring; it dealt only in generalities. So, while there is now hope for a major development in the Catholic position, there remains also the danger that the papal commission, the Pope, and the Council may produce only new verbalizations of the same old fixed ideas. This would be a severe disappointment to millions of Catholics and non-Catholics alike.

Therefore the present moment in history—the period between the third and the final sessions of the Vatican Council—is a particularly critical one, not only for Catholics but for all of us. It would be wrong to assume that only a small group of specialists on a papal commission need to be concerned with the forthcoming momentous decisions. This was underlined at the very outset of the discussion of family problems in the third session of the Council, when a group of 182 Catholic laymen from twelve learned professions (physicians, psychiatrists, jurists, philosophers, gynecologists, editors, authors, sociologists, publishers, legislators, educators, lawyers) petitioned the Pope to make a "far-reaching appraisal" of birth control teachings. They argued that, among other things, current doctrine does not take sufficient account of modern scientific developments.[63] This kind of open discussion is now more than ever an important and legitimate role for both laymen and clergy. It is partly the responsibility of non-Catholics. It is even more clearly the responsibility of liberals in the Church to keep their conscience, intelligence, and vigor turned to this problem.

Everyone who is concerned about the population explosion must hope that the Church will act on this question, not only decisively but also quickly. Yet the wish to be thorough may cause Church authorities to reflect with formidable deliberation. Some observers at the third session of the Vatican Council expressed the belief that any basic change in the Church's position would take years. Such delay may seem insignificant to prelates of a historic church in the Eternal City, but it could have disastrous social consequences.

While the Vatican is pondering its decision, there is much useful interim action that can and ought to be taken. For instance, the Rev. John A. O'Brien of the University of Notre Dame suggested, in 1963, two promising, if limited, steps: "(1) that the President call a conference at the White House for discussion of measures to help the underdeveloped nations deal effectively with their urgent population problems and (2) that the National Institutes of Health be authorized to conduct a crash research program on human reproduction in all its phases."[64] These are surely minimal and acceptable first steps in the right direction. Americans of all persuasions, non-Catholics as well as Catholics, laymen as well as the clergy, can and should support Father O'Brien's tentative and proper suggestions. And, like those Catholic professional people who petitioned the Pope in 1964, concerned individuals can and should urge the Vatican to act as promptly as possible to revaluate the Church teachings on birth control.

Chapter 6

A Time for Action

I wonder how many Americans realize that the people of Asia are just like you and me, sharing the same dreams and needs and worries. They are struggling and crying and fighting today for a bigger bowl of rice, better homes in which to live, good schools for their children, freedom from malaria and cholera and dysentery, and a place of dignity and a bit more sanity in this troubled world of ours. Either we produce quick and convincing evidence that these things can be achieved through the institutions of freedom, or the masses will turn in desperation to something else.

—LYNDON B. JOHNSON[1]

I was walking the dusty streets of a squalid Indian village with a young Delhi newspaperman. It was December, but warm. The ugly smells of poverty hung about us. Black flies were swarming on the sunny sides of buildings and humming around our ears. Grimy children were running in the streets. The newsman's face was a mixture of humiliation and hostility as he spat out his commentary: *"This* is what the British left us." Later his look changed to pride as he told me that India was now self-sufficient—in bicycles.

For all the wretchedness of people in the underdeveloped countries, theirs is nevertheless an age of hope. Many of them have attained freedom from colonial rule in the relatively short time since the end of World War II, and they are enthusiastic about the new prospect of working out their own destinies, of

107

developing their own systems of government, their own economies. As you talk with them, you can suddenly find yourself
involved in intense discussions—about new kinds of dairy farming or new methods of spinning—with intense officials whose
earnestness is almost overwhelming.

The results may not yet be impressive, judged by American
production standards; but we would be mistaken to apply only
our current standards. If we want to understand these people,
we must remind ourselves what our great-great-grandfathers were
like shortly after the United States won its own freedom: in-
tensely proud, anti-colonial, optimistic about their abilities—
and, in many villages, semi-primitive.

It is in small things like bicycles that the newly emerging
nations are taking justifiable pride, but they are important things.
They are signs of life, of economic progress in places where such
progress has been denied for centuries. Unfortunately, however,
because the populations of many of the underdeveloped countries are very large and rapidly growing, the production of food
and other material goods has not been keeping pace with the
demands of more and ever more people. India may have more
bicycles than ever before, but still only one Indian in four
hundred owns a bicycle.[2] What so recently began as an age of
hope may end in despair unless population and resources can
somehow be brought into balance. This problem will test the
ingenuity both of the underdeveloped nations themselves and of
those nations that are trying to help them emerge from poverty.

Foreign Aid and Foreign Need

> Nothing is surer than that there will
> be a decisive revolt against foreign
> aid one day if the population prob-
> lem is not faced.
> —JAMES RESTON, 1961[3]

Unfortunately, the time is past when we could hope to muddle through on such a problem. The acceleration of history is now so swift that in a single lifetime we witness social changes so varied and profound as once to have required centuries. Such speed, while exciting and promising, is perilous. Crisis has become the air we breathe, conflict our atmosphere. We have been trying to learn to accept this situation and even to turn it to use: the difference between the revolution of rising expectations and previous revolutions is that it has the applause, genuine or feigned, of all onlookers. Americans particularly tend to see themselves as backstage protagonists in this revolution—as having written part of the script for it. We have shown a creditable concern for the development of the newly emerging nations, and we have implemented that concern with our money and our skills partly because the Cold War has demanded it—and partly, as President Kennedy once said, "because it is right."

But it is one thing to join in a struggle and another thing to win it. No one who reads the statistics compiled by the United Nations agencies will conclude either that the population explosion is being slowed or that economic development is catching up with it. Since World War II, the United States has extended tens of billions of dollars in economic assistance to the underdeveloped countries: for irrigation projects, agricultural and industrial materials, gifts of food, road and factory building, and so on. Now, almost two decades after the aid programs began, Americans—including many Congressmen—have been staring at that staggering sum and asking themselves what went wrong. For the underdeveloped countries need still more roads, schools, sanitation, irrigation, hospitals, electricity, tractors, and factories. Economic development is obviously going to be slower and more expensive than the optimists had thought. The West (and particularly the United States) will be asked to do more, to approve larger and larger loans and grants of money and credit.

This is justifiable and, indeed, proper: the United States has an abundance that most Asians, Africans, and Latin Americans would find hard to believe, and not only in food. We have excess industrial potential, too much of which goes steadily unused and too much of which is producing only the fads and frills of a rich and too often self-indulgent people. We have too many bright, talented, and educated young people with no outlet for their aspirations but tawdry and humiliating occupations. We have a surplus of all consumer goods, too often only partly used and then discarded. Furthermore, part of our wealth has been acquired at the expense of the underdeveloped countries: it is their low standards of living, their cheap labor, and therefore their cheap raw materials that help to subsidize our great wealth. With respect to the underdeveloped countries, Westerners are in the position of an employer who is underpaying his employees.

It is morally right, then, that the United States assist in projects designed to create a better life for these underprivileged people. We have never done so, however, on a sufficiently large scale. The hungry people are out of sight and out of mind, and we have been content to make only rather grudging efforts toward helping them. Furthermore, Americans like to see results from even their minimal efforts. That, I take it, is why James Reston prophesied in 1961 that if the population problem were not faced soon, there would be a revolt against foreign aid.

By 1963 Reston's prophecy had already come true. The incredible expansion of population continued, and the United States government went on skittishly avoiding the economic implications of this expansion, apparently hoping that somehow the underdeveloped economies would grow faster than population. When they did not, the suspicion grew that foreign aid money was being dropped into bottomless pits. (Had not India's ambassador to the United States himself said that our economic aid had been "nullified" by population growth?) Nobody loves a loser: in 1963 Congress sharply curtailed foreign aid, even though the need was clearly for more, not less. By 1964, Congressional approval of even President Johnson's comparatively modest foreign aid bill had to be considered a "triumph."

The Necessity of Population Control

> I think there is no public in any country, once its conscience is aroused, which will fight evil with a greater sense of dedication than the public of the United States of America. I want to convince the public that overpopulation is an evil, a terrible evil.
>
> —M. C. CHAGLA[4]

When President Kennedy addressed the centennial celebration of the National Academy of Sciences in October, 1963, he said, "I particularly solicit your help in meeting a problem of universal concern: the supply of food to the multiplying mouths of our multiplying world. Abundance depends on the application of sound biological analysis to the problems of agriculture . . ."[5] The National Academy of Sciences had in fact already addressed itself to this problem and six months earlier had issued a report on it. "Nearly all our economic, social, and political problems become more difficult to solve," concluded the report, "in the face of uncontrolled population growth. . . . The desirability of limiting family size is now . . . recognized."[6]

Population control, let me repeat, is not a substitute for economic and agricultural development. But neither is the reverse true: production by itself has little chance of winning, single-handed, the race with reproduction. So both approaches are necessary, and they are complementary. The leaders of the underdeveloped countries themselves now recognize this. President Nasser of Egypt wrote in his 1962 National Charter, "Increase of population constitutes the most dangerous obstacle that faces the Egyptian people in their drive towards raising the standard of production in their country in an effective and efficient way."[7] When in the same year representatives of a large group of underdeveloped nations met in Egypt to consider their mutual problems of economic development, one of the major problems on the agenda was overpopulation. In Turkey, where the sale of contraceptives has in the past been a criminal offense, the population has doubled in the last twenty years, and in 1962 economic planners began advocating a population control policy as part of their plan for recovery. President Ayub Khan of Pakistan put the case for his country bluntly to the American people when he was in the United States a few years ago. "All the effort that is being mounted in new countries like mine will be wasted if we can't keep our population within reasonable bounds. And we look to you . . . to combat this problem."[8]

Despite all this, the United States has been, until recently, unresponsive. Asked about birth control in 1960, President Eisenhower replied, "I cannot imagine anything more emphatically a subject that is not a proper political or governmental activity or function or responsibility."[9] Certain American politicians have chided the government of India for its "neutralism"; but if we do not take up the challenge of helping the underdeveloped countries with their population problems, we are open to much the same accusation. On population limitation, Ambassador Chagla insists, "a great country like the United States cannot afford to be neutral." He is obviously not proposing that we tell other nations what they must do about their population problems, but rather that we accept the clear moral responsibility of a technologically advanced nation to try to answer such sincere and insistent pleas for help as those now coming from India. "I fail to see," says Ambassador Chagla, "how there can be any resentment or misunderstanding on the part of our Government when we ourselves realize the gravity of the situation and want to take every step to further our program . . ."[10]

What needs to be done about the population explosion in a minimum and practical way was outlined by General William H. Draper, Jr., who analyzed our foreign aid program for President Eisenhower in 1959. The United States, he reported, ought to "assist those countries with which it is cooperating in economic aid programs, *on request,* in the formulation of their plans designed to deal with the problem of rapid population growth" and "strongly support studies and appropriate research as part of its own Mutual Security Program . . ."[11]

That report, the "Draper Report," was buried under a landslide of controversy during the political campaign of 1960. Since then, populations have grown even more rapidly than before, and 250 million people have been added to the world's dinner table. It now looks as though even a broad program of population control will not be able to slow this fantastic growth in most of the underdeveloped countries within the next decade— possibly not for several decades. In fact, they will probably grow faster than ever. And the longer we put off a full-scale assault on the technical problems involved, the further off their reduction of births will have to be.

The Draper Report, though quashed at the time, nevertheless had one important effect. In the words of Arthur Krock of the *New York Times,* it (and the subsequent controversy) moved the topic of birth control "from the areas of private morals and theology into the realm of public discussion of political action. This is a result which organizations and individuals concerned with the growth of population beyond national economic capacity had been unable to achieve in years of dedication."[12]

Since the Draper Report, in fact, scores of individuals and organizations have spoken up on the subject of population control. Their suggestions for action usually center around a few simple and practical ideas:

(1) that, while the major religious institutions continue their dialogue on acceptable methods of birth limitation, governments should promote public understanding of the seriousness of the problem and the need, where it exists, for fertility control;

(2) that, as the underdeveloped nations come to understand their needs in this area, the advanced nations (individually and in the relevant United Nations agencies) develop policies and programs that will assist all nations requesting aid in population control; and

(3) that the United States in particular undertake massive re-

search in reproductive physiology and methods of fertility control, both privately (in our universities, medical schools, hospitals, and pharmaceutical firms, supported by large grants from foundations) and publicly (by Congressional and Executive action operating through our National Institutes of Health and our potential international educational forces such as the Agency for International Development and the Alliance for Progress).

Some of these programs have already been undertaken; the NIH currently assigns some three and a half million dollars annually to various kinds of reproductive studies; the National Science Foundation supports reproductive and demographic research in a number of universities; the AID is doing some educational demographic work and giving limited assistance in population control; and private organizations, from the Ford and Rockefeller Foundations to the International Planned Parenthood Federation,[13] are supporting research and education in the field. Despite these activities, however, many experts think we are not yet moving on a realistically large scale. An adequate program of research into the physiology of reproduction alone would cost, according to Dr. John Rock, a *minimum* of sixteen million dollars a year. This is three times as much as our government is now spending, and, Dr. Rock writes, "There is no private agency, or combination of agencies, which is able or willing to support a program of this magnitude. If it is to be done, it must be done by the United States government."[14]

So far, however, no branch of the United States government has yet acted vigorously in this field. The Senate Foreign Relations Committee in 1963 amended the Foreign Aid Bill to permit funds available for development research projects to be "used to conduct research into the problems of controlling population growth and to provide technical and other assistance to co-operating countries in carrying out programs of population control." But in the final version of the bill, the provision for technical assistance was deleted.

Also in the Senate in 1963, two members introduced "A Resolution to Establish a Presidential Committee on Population," charged with informing the government and the American people about population problems and recommending appropriate action. But no such committee has been appointed.

In the Executive branch, William T. Nunley, Special Assistant to Under Secretary of State Ball, suggested in 1961 that "We need technological research, physiological research, social research, economic research, and political research. We need to know more . . ."[15] Richard N. Gardner, Deputy Assistant Secretary of State for International Organization Affairs, listed, in 1963, four points of a "blueprint of a program of international cooperation *that the United States will be supporting* in the months ahead": (1) Information and Analysis, (2) Medical Research, (3) Health and Social Services, (4) The Implementation of Family Planning Programs.[16] Secretary of State Dean Rusk sent a 1963 memo to all missions of the AID stating that the United States government would be receptive to requests for assistance in population planning. President Kennedy himself, though a Roman Catholic, consistently kept an open mind on the subject of government involvement in fertility-control projects. He once declared that the "rapid, overwhelming and utterly unprecedented world population explosion" is "first among the causes" of the gap between the have and have-not nations, and he told a press conference in 1963 that research in the area of human fertility and reproduction is of great importance: "I would think," he said, "that it would be a matter which we could certainly support."[17]

Unfortunately, the Kennedy and Johnson Administrations have been hampered by a split in the ranks of their Congressional supporters (Senator J. William Fulbright and other non-Catholic Congressmen favoring research on birth control; Representative John McCormack and other Catholics against it). Action is also delayed because vested interests—religious, social, and economic—are working to obscure the problem and because the public understanding and the public conscience have not yet been sufficiently awakened. No President will push himself very far ahead of public opinion. One might argue that in a democracy, no President should; for an important program to function well in a democracy, it needs broad popular support. Unhappily, such support for population control, if it exists, is not now militant or even articulate. A Gallup Poll in 1963 revealed that almost 70 per cent of Americans had heard about the population explosion, but that only one in four thought it worth worrying about. A Louis Harris survey in 1964, reporting on what people considered to be major problems, showed a general concern for world peace, civil rights, juvenile delinquency, and other social matters, but made no mention of the population dilemma.[18]

As a move to elicit support, General Draper recently called upon the President to "follow the recommendations made publicly by various Catholic leaders that he call a White House conference of prominent Catholics, Protestants, Jews and specialists in public health, population and research." This group should "work out universally acceptable principles which can serve as a basis for settling the question of public policy—from the level of the local hospital and health departments on up to and including the U.S. position on family planning in the United Nations."[19]

Research at all levels on the physiology of reproduction is a recurring central issue. Its importance is crucial, for we know surprisingly little about this critically important subject. "A great deal is known," writes Dr. Rock, "about the mechanism whereby sperm enter the uterus in the rat, the sow, and the cow, but we have no reliable data on this process for the human species."[20] And so it is, he says, with each subdivision of the field of reproductive physiology—with sperm generation, ovulation, fertilization, and dozens of related subjects.[21]

Because of this comprehensive ignorance, present contraceptive methods are, in one scientist's words, "messy, cumbersome, inapplicable on a global scale, and in general . . . a disgrace to science."[22] A simple, cheap, and effective contraceptive does not exist. Doctors and research scientists are now investigating promising new areas. It may, for instance, be possible to improve the reliability of the rhythm method by discovering better ways of detecting ovulation. It may be possible to develop immunologic contraceptives which act by stimulating antibodies against sperm. It may be possible to discover compounds that will prevent the formation of sperm and thus serve as male birth control pills. Over the last few years there has also been a rehabilitation of older, intrauterine devices, which seem promising. They are being tested in a dozen countries, notably in Formosa, where a senior government health officer told me in 1962 that extensive experimentation had produced excellent results. They are not yet free of defects, however, and, like the present oral contraceptives, they require the attention of a doctor, which seriously limits their use in underdeveloped areas.

Alongside the problem of developing a better contraceptive is the problem of educating great masses of people to see the advantages of smaller families and therefore to use the contraceptives. This will not always be easy, because of poverty, illiteracy, superstition, and apathy. It will not be enough simply to tell peasant women that bearing too many children ultimately has evil social consequences. It will take more personal motivation to bring about reductions in birth rates. Fertility control should be introduced as an integral part of health and welfare programs. It should be associated, certainly, with the prestige of public health services, which is very high in the underdeveloped countries. It could at the same time be promoted by private businessmen, who could not only facilitate distribution of materials but also share the task of winning public acceptance of family planning. Side by side with such direct action, there would hopefully be attempts to develop new social attitudes toward, for instance, women's role in society and their opportunities to have interests outside the home. Precisely what steps might be taken, whether these or others, should of course be up to the judgment of the citizens of individual countries—but in any case, the motivations for smaller families on the part of individual parents will be most effectively influenced by concrete and practical proposals on the personal level, not by warnings (however urgent) of vast social or economic predicaments.

Another question immediately arises: just how much motivation is needed? When a contraceptive method is expensive or clumsy or otherwise unattractive, the motivation to use it must be very high indeed. A Japanese wife, advised to use a sponge-and-salt-water method, soon became disillusioned:

"Do you think it possible for us to get up in the middle of the night, especially in the cold of winter, go to the kitchen, measure out three teaspoons of salt, and prepare the solution?" Another woman complained, "You told us to wash the sponge carefully after use and dry it in the shade. Do you think this is possible without drawing the attention of curious observers?"

"What seems simple in the laboratory," commented the Japanese researcher, "is often impossible at home."[23]

In this light the often-heard pious declaration that family planning "is not a government matter" but "is up to individual families" is clearly misleading. How can this important decision be "up to" individuals until the individuals have effective means for making a choice? Granted, populations ought not to be reduced by fiat; the decision to have two or three children, rather than six or eight, should be an individual matter. But the information and public education that is required to help parents see the wisdom of smaller families is not an individual matter; it is a proper governmental function. Similarly, the development of a convenient, effective contraceptive is not an individual matter; it is now a matter for governmental concern and action. Until sufficient education and a usable contraceptive have been developed, "individual decisions" about family size will not be decisions at all; they will largely continue to be reflex actions.

John D. Rockefeller, III, who actively supports population research, has said, "The problems of population are so great, so important, so ramified and often so immediate, that only government, supported and inspired by private initiative, can attack them on the scale required."[24] Had the United States government turned its attention to this problem fifteen years ago, it might now be on the way to solution. As it is, that solution is still years in the future, and in the meantime millions of human beings continue to be unnecessarily miserable. Nor is it only our generation that will suffer from this delay. Until we come to grips with overpopulation, we are willfully condemning children of the future to unnecessary but inevitable poverty, ignorance, hunger, immorality, sickness, and early death.

"The legitimate object of government," Abraham Lincoln once said, "is to do for the people what needs to be done, but which they cannot . . . do so well, for themselves." Private sources have heretofore devoted only two or three million dollars a year for research on this problem, one of the most crucial ones of our time. Government assistance is obviously needed, but our government is only likely to take adequate action on this politically sensitive subject when two prior conditions have been satisfied: when the general public shows some active concern about it, and when the Roman Catholic Church withdraws or modifies its public opposition.

Chapter 7

Our Country and Theirs

Do generations press on generations
With no progress made?

—WORDSWORTH[1]

In 1960, in New Delhi, I was discussing population trends with Dr. Ashish Bose, an Indian research demographer. Suddenly he wrote down two figures: "1.9" and "1.7." Then he said, "India's population is growing by 1.9 per cent per year; the U.S.'s by 1.7 per cent. Why are you Americans so worried about India's problem and so unconcerned about your own?"

Dr. Bose was asking several questions at once, and there are several answers. Why is India's growth rate so ominous? Because, in the first place, India has an enormous base population. Four hundred and fifty million people increasing at 1.9 per cent per year (in 1964 it was closer to 2.2 per cent) means an enormous absolute increase of nine million people every year— as compared to less than three million in the United States. In the second place, India's population is already densely packed into its available space: approximately 370 persons per square mile—as compared to about 50 per square mile in the United States. And, perhaps most important, India's fantastic growth is flooding into a nation that cannot properly feed, clothe, educate, or provide jobs even for the people already there—as compared to the highly developed United States, where all these prospects are brighter.

Dr. Bose knew all this, of course; his point was simply that Americans should not let their comparative wealth lull them into a false sense of security. For almost two decades after World War II, the population of the United States grew at a rate comparable to that of the world as a whole. By 1963 our rate of increase had dropped somewhat, but even at the current rate of 1.4 per cent, our population would nearly double between now and the end of the century. And in 1964 the post-World War II "baby boom" generation began having its own babies—which almost certainly means that another enormous wave of population growth is on its way.

The Overdeveloped Country

> More People
> mean
> More Markets
>
> —SIGN IN THE LOBBY OF
> THE U.S. DEPARTMENT OF
> COMMERCE[2]

Businessmen have often welcomed the United States' rapidly expanding population. Vance Packard notes that the U.S. Department of Commerce labelled it a "sign of America's vigor and health," and that a business magazine maintained, "America's greatest boom is in people"; the Advertising Council circulated a picture of a stork with the caption, "This Bird Means Business"; *Printer's Ink* prophesied: "Marketing opportunities are unlimited"; and the *Engineering News Record* proposed that "The country's booming population growth spells money in the bank for the alert construction man."[3]

For any given business, such optimism may be justified—in the short run. But will the population boom in this country continue to be a blessing to business? Is it a blessing at all for most people? It can hardly give much satisfaction to our four millions of unemployed. The post-war baby boom came simultaneously with the rapid development of automation; as a result, we tend to have fewer and fewer jobs in many plants at the same time that we find ourselves with more and more potential workers. Every week, automation eliminates 25,000 jobs. Even though our economy expands rapidly enough to provide some new jobs, it has not for many years provided enough. In the five years between

1957 and 1962, almost four million persons entered the American labor force, but jobs in American private enterprise increased by only 2.2 million. We have averaged, over the last decade, 5 per cent of our working force unemployed. During the 1960's, twenty-six million new young workers will enter our labor force, and more than one-third of these will not have finished high school.[4] So the job-seekers will tend to be the young, who are undereducated and inexperienced, or the old, whose skills have become outmoded—whereas those jobs that do become available will increasingly call for high degrees of skill, training, and education.

Unemployment, then, is one of the problems that will continue to be aggravated by high birth rates, but it is not the only one. For the "overdeveloped" countries, the day is long past when a baby born one year becomes a productive member of society fifteen or so years later. The general shift of populations to cities, higher and higher educational expectations, new ideas about social welfare—all of these now make children very expensive, not only for the parents but also for society as a whole. The president of E. I. du Pont de Nemours & Co. recently wrote, with obvious concern, that "during the coming decade in the U.S. we will have to spend $1,100 to provide basic public services for every person who represents a net increase in our population."[5]

This will mean, for one thing, higher taxes. Schools and universities, hospitals and medical schools, low-cost housing, government buildings, roads, parks, and water and utility systems do not come free. All of these things—and many others—will have to be doubled within forty years. If they are not, the expansion of our population will mean that as the years go by, we shall actually become, in many important ways, a poorer nation.

This threat of poverty-amid-wealth may seem comfortably remote to some people, but not to one perceptive businessman, Adolph W. Schmidt, of T. Mellon & Sons. This is how he sees it:

Increase in per capita physical output has been declining for some time under the impact of population increase. Our gains, in other words, are increasingly nullified by the number of new hands that we must support. During the 1930's, annual increase in per capita physical output amounted to $85 for every man, woman and child in the U.S. In the war period it dropped to $59 per person; from 1945 to 1960, it dropped to $30. It is continuing to go down. In the not too distant future, we are faced with the likelihood that we will have to devote all the physical growth of our economy just to the task of standing still. *From then on, the possibility exists that a net decline in our standard of living may set in under the pressure of population.*[6]

But it is not only this problem of keeping up financially that our population explosion brings on. The expansion of our population is also destroying much of our country's irreplaceable natural beauty. Vastly increased demands for water have lowered the level of some of the Great Lakes so far that some formerly navigable bays and inlets have all but disappeared; and, as Secretary of the Interior, Stewart Udall, writes: "At the same time that our requirements for fresh water were doubling, our national sloth more than doubled our water pollution."[7] Industrial and urban wastes continue to contaminate our streams, lakes, and seasides. Strip mining is permanently destroying many miles of natural landscapes. Loggers have long since eliminated most of our vast virgin forests. Wildlife is diminishing; some species are already extinct. The efforts of our conservationists have had only belated and often limited success against these relentless by-products of population pressure. In place of "America the beautiful," we are being left more and more with floods and dust storms on the one hand, and, on the other, with urban sprawl: the megalopolis strung together along jammed and billboarded streets and highways, complete with industrial smoke, grime, and smog.

We need to bear in mind that under crowded conditions the quality of life suffers peculiar stresses and often tends to decline. As jobs get harder and harder to find, juvenile delinquency mounts; as classes get bigger, education suffers: teachers have to discipline more and end by educating less; as crowds increase, museums, libraries, parks, beaches, and other public facilities function less and less well; transportation services get so crowded that commuting becomes a degrading experience; life becomes more and more impersonal, more animalistic, less dignified. Recent tests with animals have indicated that overcrowding may even lead to mental disturbances, to social malfunctioning, and to physiological collapse.[8]

We return, then, to Professor Bose's question: Why worry

so much about India and so little about our own population explosion? A final answer is not by any means clear. In fact, it will surely become more and more obvious as time goes on that the world's population problem is not a country-by-country matter, from which certain lucky nations will be indefinitely exempt, but a world problem, which we share with all other peoples. If Americans do not see fit to develop a sensible ideal of parenthood, why should we expect Asiatic, African, or Latin American parents to do so? If we wish to be a world leader in other matters, we ought to take the lead in this field, too.

The Humanness of Human Beings

> What is a man,
> If his chief good and market of his time
> Be but to sleep and feed? A beast, no more.
> —SHAKESPEARE[9]

So, while we need to be concerned with the purely economic consequences of our population growth, we perhaps ought to consider even more seriously the question whether we are not as a nation currently making a kind of fetish of fertility, and whether consequently we are not in danger of substituting quantity for quality, procreation for creation. "A woman who cannot control her own fertility," a rebellious Catholic mother wrote in 1964, "cannot hope to be much more than a baby-machine."[10]

Having large families as a form of personal gratification is understandable. On the brighter side, it can represent a turn away from crass materialism, an act of love, a commitment to family ties, even a sign of faith in the future of one's society. That is not the whole story, though, and I sometimes wonder if there should not be a national Responsibility Committee to remind us regularly that being a parent is not necessarily being a person in one's own right—that in this crucial age requiring the intelligence and energy of a concerned citizenry, excessive fertility can be a form of self-indulgence. Reporting on American teen-age motherhood, Robert C. Cook of the Population Reference Bureau wrote in 1962: "Today, more women marry in their 18th year than in any other; more have their first child in their 19th year than in any other. At this rate, the 38-year-old grandmother will soon be a commonplace!" "Our age-at-marriage pattern," he adds, "now is closer to the Asian than to the European."[11] My hypothetical Responsibility Committee might emphasize, as a public service, that the ultimate goal of civilized society is not the mere production of greater masses, but the creation of a humane people, the creation of full and satisfying lives for mature individuals. To bring another new child into the world, it would insist, is not automatically a blessing; it *is* a great responsibility.

There was a time when it was a crucial necessity to "increase and multiply," to "fill the earth" quickly, lest famines, wars, and disease win the always touch-and-go battle for survival. Such justification no longer exists; a world growth rate of 0.5 per cent would be more conducive to human well-being than is our current 2 per cent. But to reduce the growth rate to 0.5 per cent, the two-child family will have to become the norm and a three-child family be considered large. "Under modern conditions," writes Hermann Muller, "foresight, conscience, and competence seem to express themselves rather by successful restraint in reproduction than by abundance of offspring."[12] One sometimes gets the impression that today's "reckless maternity" (as the director of the Indian census once put it) is neither an effective means to a worthwhile end, nor an end in itself, but rather a form of distraction from civilized boredom, or a tranquilizer against real and difficult external problems, or simply an attempt to prove that one is doing something to justify one's existence. Socially this adds up to bigger and more chaotic cities and countries; individually it adds up to very little. It is hardly conducive to the development of an original and profound culture, of trained intelligence, of compassion, of understanding, or of disciplined emotion.

On the contrary, what our proliferation has been encouraging is a standardized society. I do not refer simply to our tendency to buy the same cars and gadgets, wear the same clothes, listen to the same music, get the same furniture, and accept standard brands in everything. I do refer to that phenomenon which

Mill recognized a hundred years ago and which remains a threat today: the tendency to think the same thoughts, to develop the same opinions, to favor the same tastes.

It is by no means far-fetched to propose that rapid population growth plies us with more and more of this kind of standardization. In fact, those who profess not to be alarmed at the population explosion sometimes envisage a future life so different from our present one as to dismay anyone who prizes the positive, pluralistic values of our contemporary life. The Cornucopian economists, for instance, with their constant emphasis on proliferation, seem to anticipate a future life from which most of us would surely recoil in disgust, a shoulder-to-shoulder existence in which life is somehow maintained by ingenuity and industry, but only by sacrificing such things as open space and natural beauty (and even lawns and gardens), by subsisting on algae or test-tube nourishment, by curtailing freedom of movement and other freedoms as well, and by narrowing our expectations of educational, aesthetic, and emotional experience.

But man cannot live by algae alone. "The really valuable thing in the pageant of human life," wrote Albert Einstein, is "the creative, sentient individual." Life is not just a matter of cramming as many people as possible into our finite land spaces and scumming over the seas with green slime in order to feed them. For life to be human in the best sense, people must have mental well-being, or fulfillment, as Julian Huxley calls it in an eloquent passage: "understanding, enjoyment, hope, the satisfying exercise of one's faculties, creative activity, the integration of personality, participation in worthwhile projects, membership in a society which can be proud of its achievements, and a sense of significance in relation to the cosmos."[13] "We want more varied and fuller achievement in human societies," he says, "more variety and less drabness and monotony. We want more enjoyment and less suffering. We want more beauty and less ugliness. We want more adventure and disciplined freedom, as against routine and slavishness. We want more knowledge, more interest, more wonder, as against ignorance and apathy."[14]

That is an ambitious and admirable program. We would do well to remember, though, that when population growth is too rapid, it becomes a formidable obstacle to all such fulfillment.

The Pain of Being a Man

> If a nation expects to be ignorant
> and free, in a state of civilization,
> it expects what never was and
> never will be.
> —THOMAS JEFFERSON[15]

The population problem is awesomely complicated. We can arbitrarily reduce it to a matter of demographic nose-counting, or of industrial or agricultural or political theory, or of various kinds of objective sociological study; but insofar as we restrict our probing in any such way, we miss the real problem, which is to see the total demographic situation in terms of human needs and satisfactions.

Human fulfillment is an elusive goal indeed; it is, and ought to be, incapable of precise definition, impossible to stereotype. However we might disagree over details, though, Americans would probably tend to agree that fulfillment depends upon opportunities for the free exercise of our faculties: upon genuine education (as opposed to various kinds of fashionable training) and upon genuine freedom (as opposed to freedom-to-obey). In "extending to the great mass of mankind the blessings of instruction," Jefferson once wrote, "I see a prospect of great advancement in the happiness of the human race." Theologians to the contrary notwithstanding, it is precisely the idea that man can be substantially his own master, that he does bear dominion over himself, which is the basic assumption of civilized society and which is the source of our strength and—ultimately—our fulfillment.

Authoritarianism may produce an efficient, well-trained servant of the state, or of the Church. It can produce what Arthur M. Schlesinger, Jr., has called the "totalitarian man . . . ruthless, determined, extroverted, free from doubts or humility, capable of infallibility"—but this is a human cog, not a fulfilled person.

Freedom as Americans understand it depends upon education, just as true education depends upon freedom. It is precisely to avoid creating the totalitarian mentality that we dedicate our educational efforts to creating a free intelligence: to right reason, to disciplined emotion, to broad understanding—to that difficult mental equilibrium that Dr. Johnson called "the pain of being a man."

Americans like to think of themselves as champions of free choice; the education we value is therefore an education in complexities. On principle we distrust the ready-made answer, the printed catechism—knowing that if the free critical temper is compromised, there is an end to human variousness, an end to unlimited possibilities, creativity, and growth. Freedom and education for freedom are so important to us, then, because they account for the fullest development of the truly human part of our nature. But freedom is a rare thing in the history of civilizations; our own condition of freedom is far from perfect, and what we have of it is always in danger of eclipse.

What may be most ominous about our American population explosion is its direct and indirect threats to freedom as we have come to know it. How long, under fierce population pressures, can our slowly and arduously developed tolerance of human variety and individuality continue? How long, under these pressures, will our best culture, developed in thoughtfulness and leisure, survive? Freedom, it bears repeating, is an unnatural condition for mankind; it is hard to win and disturbing to possess. "Anxiety," Kierkegaard observed, "is the dizziness of freedom." When pressures are intense, the anxiety becomes intolerable and the will for freedom often diminishes; the faint-hearted waver first, but every man's determination is threatened.

As populations expand, there is a kind of physical law which erodes freedom: "The bigger the population," it reads, "the bigger the organization"—whether the organization be business, labor, or government. Harrison Brown gives us, for instance, an educated prophecy as to how future industrial organization may affect our freedom:

The industries of the future will be far more complex and highly integrated than those of today. . . . With increasing necessity and demand for efficiency, integration, and minimizing of waste in the economic world, there will be increasing demand for efficiency, integration, and minimizing of waste in the social world. . . . It seems clear that the first major penalty man will have to pay for his rapid consumption of the earth's non-renewable resources will be that of having to live in a world where his thoughts and actions are ever more strongly limited, where social organization has become all-pervasive, complex, and inflexible, and where the state completely dominates the actions of the individual.[16]

That is sinister enough, even as prophecy; but we can look about us and see the process already in operation. "The bigger the population, the bigger the government." Between 1919 and 1956, according to William Vogt, our population rose 73 per cent, but the number of people on the U.S. government payroll increased by 166 per cent.[17] Our ideas about the role of government are constantly changing: government tends to take on more and more tasks as our social consciousness evolves. For the most part, we have to approve of this, for life would be chaotic without it. But it has its darker side, too. As our population density and urbanization increase, our interdependence automatically increases proportionately. The tighter we are packed, the more regulation is required to keep us from shouldering each other too hard.

Worse, we all know that we cannot look forward to any lessening of this trend, but to the high probability of more of the same. Various proposals have been made to license childbearing, for instance, if the population explosion continues. A Catholic writer, the Rev. Anthony Zimmerman, arguing against voluntary birth control in 1961, speculated nevertheless about the possibility of future overpopulation, in the event of which "the state would be delegated as the agent to enforce uniform family limitation. More correctly, the Church would interpret the natural law in the situation, and the state would help to enforce its observation."[18] The alternatives to voluntary fertility control may one day make present infringements upon our liberties seem old-fashioned and harmless indeed.

How to Be More like Us

> I am the Almighty God . . . I will
> make my covenant between me and
> thee . . .
>   —GENESIS 17:1,2

Inhabitants of all countries tend to think of themselves as Chosen People. At Delphi, there is an enormous, elaborately carved, egg-shaped stone, the *omphalos*, supposed by the ancient Greeks to have been placed at the navel, or center, of the universe—which was, naturally, in Greece. The Greek word for any non-Greek was *barbaros*—barbarian. Similarly, Roman citizenship was an exclusive privilege, only grudgingly extended to outsiders. The Chinese have always called their great nation "the Central Kingdom," and have felt obliged to invent a myth to explain how the North Star got shifted out of its original and proper position over their heads. This ethnocentrism grows partly out of ignorance and partly out of the perfectly natural tendency for people to think themselves—and therefore their localities—important. Bostonians traditionally consider New York to be at some distance from the hub of the universe; New Yorkers only half believe in the reality of Dubuque.

In 1952, in Algeria, my wife and I shared a train compartment with two Arabs: a bright young Moroccan diesel engine operator and an ancient, muffled Algerian. We spoke French to the Moroccan, which he translated into Arabic for the old man. As we ground on through mountain and wasteland, talking, the Moroccan suddenly laughed. "I just told the old man you are from America, on the other side of the world, and he asked, 'Are there really people there?'"

The subtitle of every book, someone has said, is "How to Be More like Me." One of the implicit aims of United States foreign policy is, similarly, how to influence new nations to be as much as possible like us. Americans hope that the emerging

make the "free world" label stick to any and all non-Communists, that we have automatically gone on supporting or encouraging politically and economically despotic regimes in places like Vietnam, South Korea, Formosa, Iran, Spain, Turkey, and half a dozen Latin American countries.

This gigantic game of dog-in-the-manger with the Communists has not yielded very handsome results. The Communists appear to have been contained on most fronts, but the image of the United States in the underdeveloped countries has at the same time suffered. Talleyrand's dictum that you can do everything with bayonets except sit on them translates in the twentieth century to President Kennedy's comment, "No amount of arms and armies can help stabilize those governments which are unable or unwilling to achieve social and economic reform and development." We *know* this; but we have not been generally willing to act upon it.

The first problem for American policy makers is to recognize the socially beneficent elements in underdeveloped societies. This seems difficult in the abstract because it is so vague, but in practice it can be tied to reasonably specific criteria: to a group's or party's attitude toward such things, for instance, as land reform or living standards or public education or graft and corruption. These attitudes cannot always be analyzed with great accuracy, but they can often be seen in clear enough outline to justify making usable distinctions. Thereupon, our obligation, it seems to me, is to do our best to become allied with these progressive elements, rather than with the reactionary cliques that are often so conveniently available.

To be allied with progressive nationalists would be rather a rare experience for some American officials, but it would certainly help to improve our image abroad. Our image would also improve if we were to treat the new nations (whether democratic and capitalist or not) with the respect we ourselves wanted when we too were a weak, underdeveloped country, less than two centuries ago. Some Americans find this difficult and keep wishing aloud that the world were more tidy because more "like us"; but we shall sooner or later have to realize that, given the extraordinary stress of population pressure, our indigenous forms of democracy and capitalism are not altogether exportable—at least, not in the near future. Until we do, as a people, recognize this fact, our foreign policy will continue to operate at a disadvantage.

It is uncomfortable enough for many of us to think in terms of new socialist countries rather than new capitalist ones. It is even harder to reconcile ourselves to the new nations' authoritarianism. In the struggle between the two great power blocs, freedom is supposed, after all, to be our trump card. The American, observed Tocqueville, "is born free without having to become so"—and we therefore take it for granted not only that the emerging peoples will see liberty on our side and totalitarianism on the other, but furthermore that the attraction of liberty will be automatic and irresistible. Unfortunately, however, most of the people in most of the underdeveloped countries have never been either educated or free. They are rarely permitted a really free press, and even if they had it, most of them could not read a newspaper, much less a textbook or a bill of rights. Nor (considering current population growth rates) is all this going to change overnight. One of the most revealing and pathetic documents I came across in Asia was a newspaper story that appeared while I was in New Delhi. An educational program was being instituted there which envisioned the use of television in classrooms. The program was being delayed, however, the newspaper said, because most of the schools involved did not have electricity.

"Selling freedom" to the emerging nations, then, is not going to be a simple task. Their people often do not sufficiently feel the lack of it, and their leaders do not always think it compatible with the required social discipline. We may continue to hope that eventually, if the pressure of population growth can be eased and the economic condition of these countries improved, the "luxury" of freedom will evolve there. Indeed, this is more than a mere hope; it is one of the announced and often-repeated goals of American foreign policy. But in the meantime we ought to recognize that in our various economic alliances for progress, even allies of differing philosophies, so long as they are socially beneficent, can work together for human betterment. In fact, if we fail to work for human betterment, it is almost certain that freedom will not evolve in the new nations—not, at least, in our time.

All this is by no means a doctrine of despair. It is a doctrine of hope, but of mature and qualified, not childish and impulsive, hope. The great enemy of freedom in much of the world is poverty. If we in the wealthy West had made some effort to understand what Asian, African, and Latin American low standards of living mean in terms of human suffering—instead of concentrating so often on simply boasting about our own high one—we would not have been so surprised at the nature of the Castro revolution, for instance. We might even have created policies that would have made it less likely to have happened.

Ideology Revisited

> The conservative party . . . is timid, and merely defensive of property. It vindicates no right, it aspires to no real good, it brands no crime, it proposes no generous policy.
> —RALPH WALDO EMERSON[19]

The population explosion, then, may be generating the supreme test of our faith in ourselves. We face not only straightforward tasks, like making decisions about research in reproductive physiology (though that is central and vital). The population explosion will, sooner or later, force us to re-examine many of our social and political beliefs. The United States has suffered greatly abroad for its conservative image ("the feeble old man lecherously hugging his money-bags," as one writer has put it[20]) and for perpetuating *anciens régimes* with all their timeworn failings. Unfortunately, we are still a country too often guided (or rather, braked) by conservatives who scorn the use of intelligence in social affairs and, with "no generous policy," indeed, advise us simply to stand pat—or fight.

Thus, at a time when painstaking international negotiations have at last been rewarded by a considerable easing of world tensions, the conservative declares himself against a nuclear test ban, against disarmament, against negotiations of any kind (or even diplomatic relations) with "perfidious" governments, and even against the "part Communist" United Nations. At a time when it is increasingly clear that economic aid to underdeveloped countries is essential to avoid chaos and to contribute to the orderly development of one-third of the world, the conservative declares himself against foreign aid except in immediately and obviously self-interested situations. At a time when a spirit of nationalism and independence from Soviet domination is developing in Eastern Europe, the conservative finds his voice to speak for a freer hand with nuclear weapons, particularly for use in liberating the Communist satellites by "compelling" Soviet withdrawals.

Without reference to the facts of life in the world around them, the American conservative ideologists, fearing change, distrusting altruism, draping themselves in the hieratic wrappings of State and Church, go on preaching the virtues of unabashed, good-old-fashioned greed, declaiming against misunderstood (but clearly alien) philosophies of foreigners, and shouting in panic at the efforts of national leaders to come to grips with the real world.

Fortunately, the United States has not recently put itself wholly into the hands of the conservative ideologists. Americans have, since World War II, accepted the "mantle of free world leadership," as President Eisenhower called it, and have for the most part worn that uncomfortable cloak with whatever grace was possible. The momentous change in the American world view, from the desperate isolationism of 1940 to the relatively mature responsibility of the post-war Administrations, was far from predictable, and it is surely one of the most reassuring developments in recent history. It gives one reason to hope that what has seemed a conservative battening in this country will subside, that a philosophy of organized irresponsibility will not prevail, that we shall not fall into the easy temptation of sitting smugly amidst our H-bombs while uncontrolled population expansion drives the world relentlessly into chaos.

Our Responsibility

> Hunger allows no choice . . .
> We must love one another or die.
> —W. H. AUDEN

If the population of the world were to continue to grow at the present rate for six hundred years, there would then be only one square yard of land per person. It is inconceivable that this should happen, but the important question is: why will it not happen? Will it not happen because when population sufficiently exceeds food supplies, billions will starve to death? Or because in a desperate contest for land and food, atomic warfare will slaughter most of the human race? Or because the living standards of a tightly packed population will be reduced to such a low level that the mass killers of disease will break out again to ravage humanity?

The only way to head off such sub-human alternatives is to plan and act reasonably, without hiding behind comforting illusions—religious, economic, or political. Presumably we can be effectively concerned about threatening situations in time to prevent disaster and panic. Conservatives notwithstanding, the only way we can effectively cope with an uncertain future is by recognizing, first of all, that the world did not stop evolving in 1776 and that, fallible as our best efforts sometimes are, we can only deal with realities in a rapidly changing world, in which time is working steadily against human well-being, by committing our reason, our consciences, and our energies to the situation as it really is.

The conservative will be of no help in all this, because, as Emerson said, his stomach is full, and he cannot see why the empty stomachs of others should be of any concern to him. This is a crucial nearsightedness; in an age of diminishing distances and accelerating crises, the older, narrower concepts of self-interest have simply become obsolete. The conservative's program

—to take refuge behind national boundaries of affluence and, in case of emergency, to unleash the nuclear gunboats—is no longer an adequate response to pressing world problems. A century ago, chaos, stagnation, or aggression at the ends of the earth might not have been cause for our concern, but in the middle of the twentieth century they are directly relevant to our own national and personal security. The only conceivably secure world now is a prospering one. "If a free society cannot help the many who are poor," said President Kennedy, "it cannot save the few who are rich."[21]

Beyond the elementary and practical matter of self-interest, though, most of us recognize the claims of conscience. "Am I my brother's keeper?" was the cynicism of the world's first homicide; and the great guides of the world's conscience—Confucius, the Buddha, Jesus, Mohammed—all have answered yes to that question. Nevertheless, our stubborn egotism ("How to Be More like Us") remains; we are more concerned with minor problems in Detroit and Seattle than with major problems in Bombay and Teheran. That may serve the useful purpose of helping to solve local problems, but as a moral stance in an age of immediate mass communication and jet travel, it is no longer defensible. "Go ye into all the world" is now a genuinely practical proposal. Therefore not only is the unit of survival (as one writer has put it[22]) the human race itself; the unit of conscience should be the human race, too: we *ought* to be concerned about Bombay and Teheran. In his inaugural address, President Kennedy reminded us of the "peoples in the huts and villages of half the globe struggling to break the bonds of mass misery," and he proposed that we "pledge our best efforts to help them help themselves, for whatever period is required, not because the Communists are doing it, not because we seek their votes, but because it is right."[23]

I am aware that all this may sound bothersome and perhaps excessive. Americans, for all their tourism, are a remarkably insulated people. We may therefore find it difficult really to comprehend that our "normal" life here in the wealthy, well-fed United States, is very un-normal indeed—that for most of the world's people, life remains, as it has always been, a valley of tears. We may find it difficult to believe that the world's population is now in the act of doubling in our own lifetime, blighting attempts to improve living conditions. But those are the facts. What all the statistics mean, finally, is that the dusty children in the streets around Sealdah Station, the skinny people in the shacks and sampans of Hong Kong, the frowning refugees in mud huts in Jordan, the wretched peasants of Iran, of Brazil, of Turkey—must look to a future of little hope, unless we help them. Those people I saw in Calcutta two years ago—people with arms and legs like brittle sticks, living out their brief lives in the streets, homeless and hungry—*those people are still there.* And there are a lot more of them now than there were then.

Notes

Chapter 1

1. John Keats, "The Fall of Hyperion," 11. 154–157.
2. See Ben H. Bagdikian, *In the Midst of Plenty* (Boston, 1964), p. 176.
3. See "The President's Message," *Around the World News of Population and Birth Control*, No. 91 (Jan., 1961).
4. Edgar Snow, conversation with the author, 1961.
5. Giovanni Boccaccio, "The First Day," *The Decameron*, translated by Richard Aldington (London, 1958), p. 2.
6. *Population and Food Supply* (U.N. Office of Public Information, Basic Study No. 7), p. 2.
7. John D. Rockefeller, III, "Population: Decision by Default," *Population Bulletin*, XIX (1963), 87.
8. Julian Huxley, *The Human Crisis* (Seattle, Wash., 1963), p. 50.
9. The shifty word here is "decent"; what a decent standard of living is considered to be varies from country to country. Nevertheless, it can be discussed without being altogether arbitrary; see, e.g., Michael Harrington's guidelines in *The Other America* (Baltimore, 1963), p. 191.
10. Kamala Markandaya, *Nectar in a Sieve* (New York, 1954), p. 121.
11. Ancel Keys, Josef Brozek, Austin Henschel, Olaf Mickelsen, and Henry Longstreet Taylor, *The Biology of Human Starvation* (Minneapolis, 1950), II, 852–853.
12. Dickey Chapelle, *What's a Woman Doing Here?* (New York, 1961), p. 179.
13. *Population Profile* for March 18, 1963, issued by the Population Reference Bureau, Inc., Washington, D.C.
14. K. B. Madhava, in the New Delhi *Sunday Standard*, Jan. 6, 1963, p. 6.
15. *Population Profile*, July 6, 1964.
16. Danilo Dolci, *Report from Palermo* (New York, 1961), p. 35.
17. Tara Ali Baig, "Welfare of the Child," *Hindustan Times*, Dec. 19, 1960, p. 9.
18. *New York Times*, April 20, 1963, p. 6.
19. Margaret Mead, *Cultural Patterns and Technical Change* (New York, 1959), p. 76.

20. Arthur F. Corwin, "Mexico Resists the Pill," *The Nation*, CXCVIII (1964), 478.

21. M. C. Chagla, "A New Look at the Population Crisis," *Population Review*, V (1961), 20.

22. Joseph M. Jones, *Does Overpopulation Mean Poverty?* (Washington, 1962), p. 40.

Chapter 2

1. C. Langdon White, "Geography and the World's Population," in Stuart Mudd, ed., *The Population Crisis and the Use of World Resources* (Bloomington, Ind., 1964), p. 20.

2. For two representatives of this school of thought, see Colin Clark (*The Conditions of Economic Progress* [London, 1957] or "Do Population and Freedom Grow Together?" *Fortune*, LXXII [1960], 136–139, 203–208); and Karl Brandt (*The Reconstruction of World Agriculture* [New York, 1945] or "The Population Dilemma," *Vital Speeches of the Day*, XXIX [1963], 629–631).

3. Julian Huxley, "World Population," in C. H. Rolph, ed., *The Human Sum* (London, 1957), p. 37.

4. Huxley, *The Human Crisis*, p. 65.

5. Robert Heilbroner, *The Great Ascent* (New York, 1963), p. 111.

6. Teodoro Moscosco, "The New World of Latin America," *Saturday Review*, XLVI (Oct. 12, 1963), 27.

7. See *Population and Food Supply*, pp. 7–18.

8. Grafton D. Trout, Jr., "Urbanization and Fertility" (unpublished paper; Department of Sociology, Indiana University, 1963).

9. Garrett Hardin, quoted in Karl Sax, *Standing Room Only* (Boston, 1960), p. xiii.

10. *Around the World News of Population and Birth Control*, No. 117 (Sept., 1963).

11. Charles G. Darwin, *The Next Million Years* (London, 1952), p. 37.

12. Heilbroner, *The Great Ascent*, pp. 68–69.

13. C. M. Yonge, "Food from the Sea," in S. A. Barnett and Anne McLaren, eds., *Penguin Science Survey, 1963-B* (New York, Penguin Books, 1963), pp. 176–190.

14. Mead, *Cultural Patterns and Technical Change*, pp. 186–187.

15. Raymond Bouillenne, "Man, the Destroying Biotype," *Science*, CXXXV (Mar. 2, 1962), 706–712.

16. Harrison Brown, *The Challenge of Man's Future* (New York, 1954), p. 147.

17. See *Population and Food Supply*, p. 39.
18. Brown, *The Challenge of Man's Future*, p. 147.
19. Jonathan Garst, *No Need for Hunger* (New York, 1963), pp. 85–86.
20. W. W. Rostow, *The Stages of Economic Growth* (Cambridge, England, 1961), p. 20.
21. John P. Lewis, head of the U.S. AID mission to India, disagrees. In his *Quiet Crisis in India* (Washington, 1962), he argues that there is a considerable capacity to generate savings in India, not only among the wealthier classes but among the peasantry as well. The burden of proof of this opinion, however, seems to me to lie in the Indian economy itself, which will have to be judged by its performance. In the meantime one cannot help feeling the force of Rostow's analysis.
22. Minoru Tachi, "Population Trends and Economic Growth in Japan," paper available from the Institute of Population Problems, Ministry of Health and Welfare, Tokyo, Japan.
23. Stewart L. Udall, *The Quiet Crisis* (New York, 1963), p. 186.
24. Samuel H. Ordway, Jr., *Resources and the American Dream* (New York, 1953), p. 12.
25. William Vogt, *People!* (New York, 1961), p. 169.
26. Eugene R. Black, "Population Increase and Economic Development," in Fairfield Osborn, ed., *Our Crowded Planet* (New York, 1962), p. 90.
27. *Around the World News of Population and Birth Control*, No. 87 (Sept., 1960).
28. Heilbroner, *The Great Ascent*, p. 72.

Chapter 3

1. T. V. Ryabushkin, quoted in Philip M. Hauser, ed., *The Population Dilemma* (Englewood Cliffs, N.J., 1963), p. 145.
2. Ronald L. Meek, *Marx and Engels on Malthus* (London, 1953), p. 24.
3. *Around the World News of Population and Birth Control*, No. 91 (Jan., 1961).
4. Nikita Khrushchev, quoted in Sax, *Standing Room Only*, p. 190.
5. E. K. Federov, "We Have only Begun to Mine Our Riches," *Saturday Review*, XLV (Feb. 17, 1962), 19; and XLV (Sept. 1, 1962), 16.
6. T. V. Ryabushkin, quoted in Frank Lorimer, "Issues of Population Policy," in Hauser, ed., *The Population Dilemma*, p. 145.

7. J. D. Bernal, *Science in History* (London, 1954), p. 680.

8. Adolf Hitler, *Mein Kampf* (Munich, Germany, 1925), trans. Ralph Manheim (Boston, 1943), pp. 403-404; and *My New Order*, ed. with commentary by Raoul de Roussy de Sales (New York, 1941).

9. Vladimir Mayakovsky, "Americans Wonder," 11. 3–6, in Bernard Guilbert Guerney, ed., *An Anthology of Russian Literature in the Soviet Period* (New York, 1960), p. 39.

10. Bernard Pares, *Russia* (New York, 1962), p. 8.

11. *New York Times*, Dec. 10, 1963, p. 18.

12. Mervin Jones, "China Now," *The Observer*, May 19, 1963, p. 21.

13. William P. Bundy, "A Look Further Ahead," in *Goals for Americans* (New York, 1961), p. 365.

14. Private conversation with an American demographer in Moscow, 1963.

15. Czeslaw Milosz, *The Captive Mind* (New York, 1955), p. 51.

16. Correspondence in *Saturday Review*, XLV (Sept. 1, 1962), 15.

17. Sax, *Standing Room Only*, p. 191.

18. Confucius, *Analects*, Book II, Chapter XIII.

19. Richard Dudman, "Communist China from the Rim," *The Progressive*, XXVII (May, 1963), 19.

20. Edgar Snow, *The Other Side of the River* (New York, 1962), p. 415.

21. *Around the World News of Population and Birth Control*, No. 117 (Sept., 1963).

22. Edgar Snow, "A Chat with Chou-En-lai," *Chicago Sun-Times*, Feb. 23, 1964, II, 2.

23. Karl Marx and Friedrich Engels, *The Communist Manifesto*, Authorized English Translation (New York, 1948), p. 24.

24. Stanislas de Lestapis, S.J., *La Limitation des naissances* (Paris, 1960), pp. 23–24; Vera Houghton, "Why Family Planning?" (unpublished memorandum, International Planned Parenthood Federation), p. 29.

25. Richard N. Gardner, "The Politics of Population: A Blueprint for International Cooperation," in Mudd, ed., *The Population Crisis and the Use of World Resources*, p. 355.

26. Ayub Khan, quoted by James Reston in the *New York Times*, July 21, 1961.

27. John S. Aird, "Population, Planning, and Economic Development in Mainland China in a Decade of Crisis," *Population Bulletin*, XIX (1963), 133.

28. Dolci, *Report from Palermo*, p. 49.

29. Robert C. Cook, "World Food Supply," *Population Bulletin,* XV (Feb., 1959), 1.

Chapter 4

1. Msgr. John Romaniello, *Bird of Sorrow;* published in paperback as *Escape from Red China* (New York, n.d.), p. 7.
2. Msgr. John C. Knott, correspondence in *America,* CIX (1963), 225.
3. Sophocles, *Antigone,* Ode I, Strophe 1, English version by Dudley Fitts and Robert Fitzgerald, *The Oedipus Cycle* (New York, 1949).
4. Pius XI, *On Christian Marriage,* para. 56.
5. Max Caspar, *Kepler* (London and New York, 1959), pp. 377, 88.
6. Joseph Duhamel, in *America;* quoted in the *New York Times,* August 8, 1963, p. 12.
7. John Courtney Murray, S.J., "Natural Law and Public Consensus" in John Cogley, ed., *Natural Law and Modern Society* (New York, 1962), p. 57.
8. Pius XI, *On Christian Marriage,* para. 108.
9. Correspondence in *America,* CVIII (1963), 728.
10. Charles E. Morton, "What Protestants Think about Natural Law," *Catholic World,* CXC (1960), 299.
11. Statement adopted by the General Board of the National Council of Churches of Christ in the U.S.A., Feb. 23, 1961; distributed by the Planned Parenthood Federation of America, Inc., New York.
12. Morton, "What Protestants Think about Natural Law," p. 297.
13. James A. Pike, "A Protestant's View," in Osborn, ed., *Our Crowded Planet,* p. 199.
14. Reinhold Niebuhr, "A Plea for Tolerance," *Atlantic Monthly,* CCX (1962), 76.
15. A. D. White, *A History of the Warfare of Science with Theology in Christendom* (New York, 1960), II, 31–32, 55.
16. Paul Quay, S.J., "Contraception and Conjugal Love," *Theological Studies,* XXII (1961), 18.
17. *Ibid.,* p. 34; emphasis added.
18. Philip Selznick, "Natural Law and Sociology," in Cogley, ed., *Natural Law and Modern Society,* p. 181.
19. White, *A History of the Warfare of Science with Theology in Christendom,* I, 117.

20. *Ibid.*, I, 137.

21. *Ibid.*, I, 145–146; emphasis added.

22. Brand Blanshard, quoted by Robert Gordis, "Natural Law and Religion," in Cogley, ed., *Natural Law and Modern Society*, p. 247.

23. John Stuart Mill, "Nature," in George Nakhnikian, ed., *Nature and Utility of Religion* (Indianapolis and New York, 1958), pp. 20–21.

24. *Ibid.*, p. 22.

25. The Buddha, from the Proverbs of *The Dhammapada*, in Robert O. Ballou, ed., *The Portable World Bible* (New York, 1944), p. 140.

26. Arthur McCormack, *Overpopulation—Is Birth Control the Answer?* (London: Catholic Truth Society, 1960), p. 17.

27. Alvah Sulloway, *Birth Control and Catholic Doctrine* (Boston, 1959), pp. 108–112.

28. William Lillie, *An Introduction to Ethics* (London, 1961), pp. 65, 290.

29. *New York Times*, May 6, 1963, p. 9.

30. Anne Biazanek, correspondence in *Family Planning*, XII (1964), 104.

31. Rosemary Reuther, "A Catholic Mother Tells 'Why I Believe in Birth Control,'" *Saturday Evening Post*, April 4, 1964, p. 12.

32. Michael Novak, "Marriage: the Lay Voice," *Commonweal*, LXXIX (1964), 590.

33. Chagla, "A New Look at the Population Crisis," *loc. cit.*, p. 21.

34. Pope Pius XII, quoted by Bruce Martin Russett, "Some Unpleasant Facts about Population Pressures," *America*, CVII (1962), 1125.

35. Dolci, *Report from Palermo*, p. 115.

36. *Ibid.*, p. 227.

37. *Around the World News of Population and Birth Control*, No. 111 (Jan., 1963).

38. Baig, "Welfare of the Child," p. 9.

39. John A. O'Brien, "Let's End the War over Birth Control," *The Christian Century*, LXXX (1963), 1361.

40. Lestapis, *La Limitation des naissances*, p. 261.

41. Donald Attwater, ed., *A Catholic Dictionary* (New York, 1949), p. 20; emphasis added.

42. Quoted in Paul Blanshard, *American Freedom and Catholic Power* (Boston, 1959), p. 331.

43. John A. Ryan and Francis J. Boland, *Catholic Principles of Politics* (New York, 1952), pp. 162–163.

44. Pope Pius XI, quoted in W. J. Gibbons, "Fertility Control in the Light of Some Recent Catholic Statements," *Eugenics Quarterly,* III (1956), 10.

45. O'Brien, "Let's End the War over Birth Control," p. 1362.

46. *The Christian Century,* LXXVIII (1961), 1293.

47. *New York Times,* May 2, 1963, p. 34.

48. *New York Times,* Sept. 7, 1962, p. 25; and Sept. 8, 1962, pp. 1, ff.; see also *A Survey of Research on Reproduction Related to Birth and Population Control (as of January 1, 1963),* Public Health Service Publication No. 1066.

49. Louisville *Courier-Journal,* April 18, 1964, I, 14.

50. *America,* CVI (Nov. 4, 1961), 148; emphasis added.

51. Letter to *Family Planning,* XI (1962), 69.

52. Speech by Julian Antonio Alvarado, reported in *Religious News Service,* April 23, 1964.

53. Barbara Cadbury, "Family Planning in East Asia," in Barnett and McLaren, eds., *Penguin Science Survey, 1963-B,* p. 107.

54. *The Christian Century,* LXXVIII (1961), 1196–1197.

55. Brock Chisholm, quoted by Karl Sax, "The World's Exploding Population," *Perspectives in Biology and Medicine,* VII (1963–1964), 326–327.

56. Francis Bacon, from the essay "Of Great Place."

57. Norman St. John-Stevas, *Life, Death, and the Law* (Bloomington, Ind., 1961), p. 96.

58. *Commonweal,* LXXVIII (1963), 272.

59. See *The New Republic,* CXLIII (Dec. 7, 1960), 6.

60. See Blanshard, *American Freedom and Catholic Power,* p. 322.

61. "A Talk to Catholic Wives" [pamphlet by "A Catholic Woman Doctor"], (London: Catholic Truth Society, 1959), p. 26.

62. Private report to the author by a U.S. embassy official while in Poland.

63. *America,* CIV (1961), 789; CV (1961), 733.

64. Carl Becker, *Freedom and Responsibility in the American Way of Life.*

65. "A Talk to Catholic Wives," p. 4.

66. Lestapis, *La Limitation des naissances,* p. ii.

67. Quay, "Contraception and Conjugal Love," p. 35.

68. Blanshard, *American Freedom and Catholic Power,* p. 216.

69. Kenneth Underwood, *Protestant and Catholic* (Boston, 1961), p. 153.

70. *New York Times,* May 6, 1963, p. 9.

71. *New York Times*, April 1, 1963, p. 14.
72. *New York Times*, March 16, 1964, p. 3.
73. *Around the World News of Population and Birth Control*, No. 72 (Feb., 1959).
74. Cardinal Désiré Joseph Mercier, *The Duties of Married Life* (London: Catholic Truth Society, 1960), pp. 2–3.
75. *New York Times*, Aug. 8, 1963, p. 12.
76. G. P. Dwyer, *Birth Control* (London: Catholic Truth Society, 1959), p. 3.
77. Associated Press report, Oct. 9, 1963; see *Population Bulletin*, XIX (1963), p. 207.
78. *America*, CVIII (1963), 662.

Chapter 5

1. *New York Times*, Aug. 8, 1963, p. 12.
2. Arthur M. Schlesinger, Jr., *The Vital Center* (Boston, 1949), p. 82.
3. Bertrand L. Conway, C.S.P., *The Question Box* (New York, 1929), pp. 112–113; emphasis added.
4. *Around the World News of Population and Birth Control*, No. 112 (Feb., 1963); emphasis added.
5. James W. Brackett and Earl E. Huyk, "The Objectives of Government Policies on Fertility Control in Eastern Europe," *Population Studies*, XVI (1962), 135.
6. Richard Crossman, ed., *The God that Failed* (New York, 1949), pp. 20, 47.
7. Snow, "A Chat with Chou-En-lai," p. 2; emphasis added.
8. Richard N. Gardner, "The Politics of Population," in Mudd, ed., *The Population Crisis and the Use of World Resources*, p. 355.
9. Brackett and Huyk, "The Objectives of Government Policies on Fertility Control in Eastern Europe," p. 139.
10. Appleman, Philip, "What the Population Explosion Means to You," *Ladies Home Journal*, June, 1963, pp. 59 ff.
11. Brackett and Huyk, "The Objectives of Government Policies on Fertility Control in Eastern Europe," p. 139.
12. Lee Rainwater, *And the Poor Get Children* (Chicago, 1960), p. 47.
13. Robert C. Cook, "Low Birth Rates of European Catholic Countries," *Population Bulletin*, XVIII (1962), 21–39.
14. Beric and Joyce Wright, "The First Family Planning Clinic in Trinidad," *Family Planning*, V (1957), 9.
15. Houghton, "Why Family Planning?" p. 18.

16. *New York Times,* Oct. 22, 1960, p. 1; Oct. 23, 1963, p. 42; Oct. 24, 1963, p. 1; Oct. 29, 1963, p. 1; Nov. 4, 1963, p. 25; Nov. 22, 1963, p. 1.
17. *Around the World News of Population and Birth Control,* No. 92, Feb., 1961.
18. John Rock, *The Time Has Come* (New York, 1963), p. 41.
19. "The Harris Survey," Louisville *Courier-Journal,* Feb. 10, 1964, I, 8.
20. Rainwater, *And the Poor Get Children,* p. 35.
21. *Ibid.,* p. 39.
22. *Commonweal,* LXXX (1964), 311.
23. Raymond J. de Martini, *The Right of Nations to Expand by Conquest* (Washington, 1947), p. 80.
24. McCormack, "Overpopulation—Is Birth Control the Answer?" pp. 12, 5.
25. Dwyer, *Birth Control,* p. 21.
26. Lestapis, *La Limitation des naissances,* p. 249.
27. Dwyer, *Birth Control,* p. 14; Quay, "Contraception and Conjugal Love," p. 39.
28. Justin McCann, *Self-Discipline* (London: Catholic Truth Society, 1960), p. 5.
29. Henry Noel Brailsford, *Subject India* (London, 1943), p. 124.
30. *Commonweal,* LXXVI (1962), 270.
31. *Ibid.,* p. 424.
32. Bruce Martin Russett, "The Catholic and the Population Problem," *Catholic World,* CXCV (1962), 1125.
33. *America,* XVII (1962), 765.
34. John E. Dunsford, "Public Policy on Birth Control," *America,* CXI (1964), 133.
35. *New York Times,* Aug. 6, 1963, p. 16.
36. *Ibid.*
37. Blanshard, *American Freedom and Catholic Power,* p. 331.
38. Melvin G. Shimm and Robinson O. Everett, eds., *Population Control* (Duke University, 1961), pp. 71–72.
39. See, e.g., Herbert Ratner, "The Rock Book—A Catholic Viewpoint," *Commonweal,* LXXVIII (1963), 392–395.
40. *New York Times,* Aug. 6, 1963, p. 16.
41. *The Criterion* (diocesan newspaper, Indianapolis, Ind.), June 5, 1964, pp. 1, 9.
42. Hans Küng, "The Church and Freedom," *Commonweal,* LXXVIII (1963), 344–345, 347.

43. Gustave Weigel, S.J., "The Church and the Public Conscience," *Atlantic Monthly*, CCX (1962), 118–119.

44. George W. Cornell, "Catholics Seek to Lower Obstacle of Infallibility," Louisville *Courier-Journal*, Oct. 5, 1963, p. 15.

45. *New York Times*, Nov. 9, 1963, p. 2.

46. Pius XI, *On Christian Marriage*, para. 16.

47. "Statement by His Holiness Pope Pius XII," *Eugenics Review*, XLVII (1955–1956), 6; *Vegliare con sollecitudine*, para. 36.

48. John A. O'Brien, "Family Planning in an Exploding Population," *The Christian Century*, LXXX (1963), 1050.

49. *Ibid.*, p. 1051.

50. *Ibid.*, p. 1052.

51. *Around the World News of Population and Birth Control*, No. 112 (Feb., 1963).

52. Robert I. Gannon, "A Roman Catholic Speaks," in Osborn, ed., *Our Crowded Planet*, p. 193; emphasis added.

53. Attwater, ed., *A Catholic Dictionary*, p. 151.

54. E. Schillebeeckx, "Procreation and Human Dignity," *Commonweal*, LXXX (1964), 332.

55. Rock, *The Time Has Come*, p. 60; emphasis added.

56. White, *A History of the Warfare of Science with Theology in Christendom*, II, 60.

57. Schillebeeckx, "Procreation and Human Dignity," p. 332.

58. *The Criterion*, June 26, 1964, p. 9.

59. *Los Angeles Times*, Oct. 30, 1964, I, 3, 23.

60. *Los Angeles Times*, Oct. 31, 1964, I, 7.

61. *Los Angeles Times*, Oct. 30, 1964, I, 23.

62. *The Criterion*, June 26, 1964, p. 9.

63. *New York Times*, Oct. 20, 1964, p. 1.

64. O'Brien, "Let's End the War over Birth Control," p. 1364.

Chapter 6

1. Lyndon B. Johnson, "A Bigger Bowl of Rice," *Parade*, Aug. 13, 1961, p. 4.

2. Heilbroner, *The Great Ascent*, p. 111.

3. *New York Times*, July 21, 1961, p. 22.

4. M. C. Chagla, "The Population Crisis in India" in Mudd, ed., *The Population Crisis and the Use of World Resources*, p. 154.

5. Louisville *Courier-Journal*, Oct. 23, 1963, p. 6.

6. "The Growth of World Population," *Population Bulletin*, XIX (1963), 105–106.

7. *Around the World News of Population and Birth Control*, No. 107 (Sept., 1962).

8. *Annual Report* for 1961, Population Reference Bureau, p. 17.

9. *New York Times*, Dec. 3, 1959, p. 1. (Later he changed his mind; see the *Saturday Evening Post* for October 26, 1963.)

10. Chagla, "A New Look," pp. 20–21.

11. *Composite Report of the President's Committee to Study the United States Military Assistance Program* (Washington, 1959), I, 96–97; emphasis added.

12. *New York Times*, Dec. 1, 1959, p. 38.

13. The voluntary agencies welcome the support of interested individuals. The address of the International Planned Parenthood Federation is: 64 Sloane St., London, S.W.1, England. The address of Planned Parenthood-World Population Emergency Campaign is: 501 Madison Ave., New York 22, N.Y., U.S.A.

14. Rock, *The Time Has Come*, pp. 196–199.

15. William T. Nunley, Address to the National Conference on International Economic and Social Development (Washington, D.C., Dec. 1, 1961), *Department of State Bulletin*, XLVI (1962), 24.

16. Richard N. Gardner, "The Politics of Population," *Saturday Review*, XLVI (1963), 38; emphasis added.

17. Joseph M. Jones, p. 37; *New York Times*, April 25, 1963, p. 16.

18. "Harris Survey," Louisville *Courier-Journal*, June 22, 1964, I, 7.

19. William H. Draper, Jr., "Birth Control: The Problem We Fear to Face," *Look*, XXV (Dec. 5, 1961), 44.

20. Rock, *The Time Has Come*, 197.

21. *Ibid.*, 198.

22. A. S. Parkes, "Contraception in Its Modern Context," in Barnett and McLaren, eds., *Penguin Science Survey*, p. 85.

23. Yoshio Koya, "Lessons from Contraceptive Failure," *Population Studies*, XVI (1962), 4–11.

24. Draper, "Birth Control: The Problem We Fear to Face," p. 44.

Chapter 7

1. William Wordsworth, *The Excursion*, V, 466–467.

2. Vance Packard, "Progress through Proliferation?" in Marian Maury, ed., *Birth Rate and Birth Right* (New York, 1963), p. 157.

3. *Ibid.*, pp. 158–159.

4. B. J. Widick, *Labor Today* (Boston, 1964), p. 26.

5. Statement by Lammot du Pont Copeland; available from the Planned Parenthood Federation of America, 501 Madison Ave., New York 22, N.Y.

6. Statement available from the Planned Parenthood Federation of America (see note 5).

7. Udall, *The Quiet Crisis*, p. 176.

8. *New York Times*, Sept. 22, 1963, p. 79.

9. William Shakespeare, *Hamlet*, V, iv.

10. Reuther, "A Catholic Mother Tells 'Why I Believe in Birth Control,'" p. 14.

11. *Population Profile* for June 2, 1962 and June 1, 1964; issued by the Population Reference Bureau, Washington, D.C.

12. Hermann J. Muller, "Better Genes for Tomorrow," in Mudd, ed., *The Population Crisis and the Use of World Resources*, p. 315.

13. Julian Huxley, "Population Planning and Quality of Life," in *Report of the Proceedings*, the Sixth Annual Conference on Planned Parenthood (London, n.d.), p. 22.

14. Huxley, "Too Many People!" in Osborn, *Our Crowded Planet*, pp. 224–225.

15. From a letter to Colonel Yancey, 1816.

16. Brown, *The Challenge of Man's Future*, pp. 218–219.

17. Vogt, *People!* p. 66.

18. Anthony F. Zimmerman, *Catholic Viewpoint on Overpopulation* (New York, 1961), pp. 190–191.

19. Ralph Waldo Emerson, "New England Reformers."

20. Ivor Kraft, "Decadent Conservatism and Fighting Liberalism," *The Humanist*, XXII (1962), 21.

21. John F. Kennedy, "Inaugural Address," Jan. 20, 1961.

22. Hudson Hoagland, "The Unit of Survival Is the Human Race," in Mudd, ed., *The Population Crisis and the Use of World Resources*, pp. 442–450.

23. John F. Kennedy, "Inaugural Address."

Index

153